EARLY READERS CATCH THE WORMS

HOW ALPHA, BETA, AND ARC READERS CAN HELP YOU PUBLISH A BETTER NOVEL

CAROL BETH ANDERSON

CONTENTS

Introduction	1
PART 1 **ALPHA READERS**	
How Not to Form an Alpha Reader Group	13
Alpha Reader Overview	16
Where to Find Alpha Readers If You Don't Have a Fan Base	19
Where to Find Alpha Readers If You Have a Fan Base	22
Pros and Cons of Asking Fellow Authors to Be Early Readers	25
How to Invite Someone to Be an Alpha Reader	28
How to Organize Your Alpha Reader Group	31
How Often to Request Feedback from Alpha Readers	37
Formatting a Manuscript for Your Early Readers	40
Providing Book Files to Readers	43
Requesting Feedback from Alpha Readers	45
How to Encourage Alpha Reader Follow-Through	49
Responding to Feedback	52
Deciding Which Feedback to Utilize When Revising	55
How to Organize Feedback	57
How to Know When the Alpha Reader Phase is Complete	60
Removing Inactive Group Members	62
Adding New Group Members	64
Don't Get Lost in Your Drafting Cave	66
The Alpha Reader Phase: Make it Your Own	68

PART 2
BETA READERS

Beta Reader Overview	73
Pre-Beta Step 1: Polish Up That Manuscript!	75
Pre-Beta Step 2: Format and Choose How to Distribute Your Manuscript Files	79
Pre-Beta Step 3: Create an Application	80
Pre-Beta Step 4: Create a Feedback Form	85
Where to Find Beta Readers	90
How to Ask for Beta Readers	93
Choosing Your Beta Readers	97
Communicating With Beta Applicants Who Don't Make the Team	101
Welcoming Your New Beta Readers	104
The Key to Beta Reader Follow-Through	109
Responding to Beta Feedback	114
Organizing and Evaluating Beta Feedback and Revising Your Manuscript	116
How to Know Your Post-Beta Revisions Are Done	118
The Beta Reader Phase: Make it Your Own	120

PART 3
ARC READERS

ARC Readers Overview	125
Pre-ARC Step 1: Make Your Book Shine	128
Pre-ARC Step 2: Review Sites	130
Pre-ARC Step 3: Organize Your Links	134
Pre-ARC Step 4: Formatting Your ARC	136
Pre-ARC Step 5: Choose a Distribution Service	139
Pre-ARC Step 6: Set Up Review Reporting	144
How Big an ARC Team Should Be	146
How to Find ARC Readers	148
Choosing Your ARC Readers	155
How to Ask for ARC Readers	157
Communicating With ARC Readers	161
Asking Your ARC Readers to Report Typos	167
The ARC Reader Phase: Make it Your Own	170

PART 4
QUESTIONS & ANSWERS

Q&A: Start Here	175
Help! What If I'm Overwhelmed?	177
Where Do Editors Fit in My Process?	178
Do Early Readers Replace Editors?	182
What If No One Wants to Read My Book?	185
What If My Alpha or Beta Readers Aren't Giving Me Feedback?	187
What If My ARC readers Aren't Leaving Reviews?	190
Do I Need Sensitivity Readers?	192
When Is It Time to "Fire Someone" From an Early Reader Team?	195
Should Alpha and/or Beta Readers Review My Finished Book?	197
What If I Feel Guilty Asking People to Help Me?	199
How Do I Get Over My Fear of Feedback?	201
Will Early Readers Steal My Book?	204
Can I Send My Book to ARC Readers After It's Published?	207
How Can I Thank My Early Readers?	209
Conclusion	211
Appendix 1: Story Structure Resources	213
Appendix 2: File Formatting Options	215
Appendix 3: A Sample Early Reading, Revision, and Editing Process	221
Appendix 4: Self-Editing and Revision Resources	223
Appendix 5: Useful Websites	225
Acknowledgements	233
About the Author	235

Early Readers Catch the Worms by Carol Beth Anderson

Published by
Eliana Press
P.O. Box 2452
Cedar Park, TX 78630

www.carolbethanderson.com

Copyright © 2021 by Carol Beth Anderson

All rights reserved. No portion of this book may be reproduced in any form without permission from the publisher, except as permitted by U.S. copyright law. For permissions contact:
beth@carolbethanderson.com

Cover Design:
Carol Beth Anderson

Paperback ISBN: 978-1-949384-08-6

First Edition

To all my alpha, beta, and ARC readers. You make me a better writer.

INTRODUCTION

It's finally happening, I told myself. *My beta readers are flaking on me.*

I'd sent my beta reader team a novel manuscript, giving them a month to read it and send me feedback. They'd had the book for a few weeks, and I was still waiting to hear from a lot of them.

Maybe I'd gotten overconfident. Maybe my communication system didn't work as well as I thought. Still, I kept with it, sending my betas regular reminders.

As the deadline approached, feedback flew in. In the end, twenty-six out of twenty-eight of my betas—93%—provided me with feedback. The two others had understandable reasons for backing out, and they both agreed to be ARC readers (early reviewers) instead of betas.

It was my seventh fiction book and my best beta follow-through ever.

I can't promise that if you follow my system, nine out of ten of your betas will give you feedback. **All authors are different; every book is unique.** Your experience won't mirror mine (and building a reliable team takes time).

I'm also not going to advise you work with twenty-eight beta readers; I tend to go overboard! (We'll cover how many readers you need later.)

Here's what I *will* promise you: **this book is full of practical advice for building and optimizing your early reader systems.**

Let's dive in.

WHAT THIS BOOK INCLUDES

My goal is to give you a practical, usable guide to working with early readers, in a compact format. I'll move quickly so you can get back to doing what you love: writing stories.

The book is organized into four major parts:

1. Alpha Readers
2. Beta Readers
3. ARC Readers
4. Questions & Answers

Each part is broken into easily digestible topics. These aren't quite chapters—some are less than a page long, while others go into much more depth. You'll find a short summary at the end of each topic, to help you focus on what's most important.

If you're the type who likes to hop around when you read a how-to book, you can easily navigate to the specific topic you need through the Table of Contents.

At the end of the book are five Appendices with resources for those who want to go deeper.

In the book's digital version, you'll see lots of internal links that will help you jump to information throughout the book (for instance, an Appendix or a previous chapter that relates to the current topic). In the hard-copy version, you'll find page-number references instead of links.

Some of the information in this book is subject to change (such as websites that discontinue or modify their author services). You can review post-publication changes at this link:

carolbethanderson.com/updates

WHAT THIS BOOK DOESN'T INCLUDE

Early reader processes are related to many other aspects of writing and publishing, including (but not limited to):

- Planning/outlining
- Revision, self-editing, and professional editing
- Marketing (social media, forming and maintaining a newsletter, etc.)

All these topics are important. However, if I covered them in deep detail, this book might turn into a tome the length of *War and Peace*. Instead of trying to cover all these peripheral subjects, I'll guide you along the way to resources written by experts. That way, you'll know where to turn for the information you need.

WHAT EARLY READERS ARE AND WHY YOU NEED THEM

I titled this book *Early Readers Catch the Worms*. For the purposes of this book, **early readers are alpha, beta, and ARC readers**.

Those terms—*alpha, beta,* and *ARC readers*—are kind of like biscuits. Stick with me here. (Oh, who am I kidding? If you're anything like me, you'll definitely stick around for biscuits.)

If you speak British English, the word *biscuit* may conjure an image of a flat, sweet, crunchy treat—what those in the United States would call a *cookie*.

I've always lived in the US, and when I hear the word *biscuit*, I think of a round, fluffy breakfast bread, brown on top and soft inside. Biscuits are perfect eaten hot with butter (and maybe honey or jam). I also love them with gravy . . . another word with a variety of meanings.

Our definitions of *biscuit* vary depending on our backgrounds. Similarly, authors use different definitions of *alpha readers, beta readers,* and *ARC readers,* according to their experiences. Here's how I define the various types of early readers:

First of all, **early readers are *readers***. I know that's obvious, but here's what I mean: they aren't necessarily fellow writers. They can be, but more importantly, early readers should enjoy reading in your genre. The more closely an early reader aligns with your target audience, the more likely they are to give useful feedback or relevant reviews.

An **alpha reader** reads an early version of your manuscript, often in sections. They give big-picture feedback on your book, addressing elements such as plot, characters, and pacing. By fixing those issues at an early stage, you'll set yourself up for success as you continue to write and revise.

You may be thinking, *That sounds like a critique partner.* However, critique partners are usually fellow writers, while alpha readers may not be. Also, critique partners often exchange manuscripts with each other, and that's not necessarily the case with alpha readers.

A **beta reader** reads a revised, somewhat polished version of your full manuscript. They may give big-picture feedback or detail-centric feedback or both (depending on the reader, the book, and what the author requests). Betas are priceless. Their feedback helps authors turn good books into great books.

An **ARC reader** reads an ARC (Advance Review Copy) of your complete, spit-polished book shortly before publication. They give the *world* feedback by reviewing it, which can give the book more credibility to prospective readers. Some ARC readers may even catch last-minute typos for you.

Back to our title, *Early Readers Catch the Worms.* We've talked about what early readers are, but what are worms?

WORMS

Ever bitten into an apple that looked nice on the outside . . . glossy, red, suitable for a teacher's desk . . . and found a worm or other disgusting bug inside? Did you spit out your bite and toss the fruit in the trash?

Worms are the annoying elements that creep into our novels, making readers want to spit out our words and throw our books in the garbage (or trash them in Goodreads reviews).

Here's an example of a worm in a novel. The other day, I was reading through the first draft of the novel I'm working on. I found this:

"Her stomach curved into a nervous smile."

That sentence is a wriggly, slimy worm. I'm all for a good metaphor, but that one took it too far. I'm still trying to figure out how my "drafting brain" came up with it.

Manuscripts contain all sorts of other worms that can keep readers from staying engaged. They could be **structural, plot, or character related**. Then there are **grammar, style, spelling, and formatting** worms.

It's great when we find worms on our own. I was glad to find my "stomach smiling" worm in my first draft. However, all too often, we gloss right over our own worms.

Here's the good news: *Early Readers Catch the Worms*. Alpha, beta, and ARC readers won't make your novel perfect (no such thing), but they'll catch many of the nasty little—and big—annoyances that might turn off your readers.

Effective teams of early readers will help you catch your worms and publish better novels.

WHO THIS BOOK IS WRITTEN FOR

If you're a novelist who wants to produce a shiny, polished story instead of a worm-filled mess, I wrote this book with you in mind. Much of the advice applies to nonfiction too, but some of it will be specific to fictional works like novels and novellas.

More specifically, *Early Readers Catch the Worms* will be most helpful for these types of novelists:

- Those pursuing **self-publishing**. I'm a self-published author, so this book is packed with advice for others like me who make all their own publishing decisions.
- Those pursuing publishing with a **very small, indie press** that gives them many of the same freedoms self-

published authors have. If that describes you, you'll be able to implement much of the advice in this book. However, parts of it may not apply to you. (For instance, your publisher may have specific requirements for your ARC phase.)
- Those **hoping to find an agent.** If you're in this category, focus on the sections on alpha and beta reading. Those parts are designed to help you write a better book (which will hopefully catch the attention of agents you query). The ARC section probably won't apply to you if you find that coveted agent and publisher. (A well-established, larger publisher will have their own marketing plan.)

What about authors who are already agented and/or working with large traditional publishers? First, congratulations on making it so far in your publishing journey! You may find some parts of this book to be useful. However, much of my advice may not fit with your agent's and publisher's editorial and marketing processes.

A NOTE IF YOU'RE HESITANT TO SHOW YOUR WRITING TO OTHERS

You probably picked up this book because you believe in the value of getting feedback and reviews. However, you may also be hesitant to hand over your unpublished words to early readers. If so, feel free to check out one or both of these topics (from the Q&A section near the end of the book) before moving forward:

- How Do I Get Over My Fear of Feedback? (p. 201)
- Will Early Readers Steal My Book? (p. 204)

If you're still struggling with the idea of sharing, take baby steps! You can implement the ideas in this book with teams that are as small as you like. One trusted alpha or beta reader is better than none!

Once you're ready to share your work with others, some of my advice still may not resonate with you. That's why I encourage you to . . .

MAKE THIS BOOK YOUR OWN

Time for a true confession.

I dog-ear the pages of my books. I've also been known to break the spines of paperbacks, drop books in the bathtub, and write notes in the margins. When I switched over to reading primarily on Kindle, book purists across the world doubtless breathed a collective sigh of relief. But I've never felt the need to baby my books. It's the words on the pages that matter, not the pages themselves.

The book in your hands isn't a classic work of literature, bound in soft leather. **It's a tool.** Enjoy reading it! Beat it up, figuratively or literally. Take notes. Hop from one part of the book to another. Duplicate my systems exactly, or adjust them to fit you. At the end of each of the three major sections, I'll even give you suggestions on how to "Make it Your Own."

HOW NOT TO REINVENT THE WHEEL

While I want you to customize these processes, I also want to make it easy for you to follow my methods when they work for you.

Throughout this book, I'll give you templates for communicating with your early readers, including the following:

- Alpha reader instructions
- Beta reader application
- Beta reader feedback form
- ARC instructions for the beginning and end of a book
- ... and many more.

I've put all these resources into easily duplicated, editable formats so you don't have to create them from scratch. To get your resource pack, sign up for my Author Resources newsletter at the following link:

carolbethanderson.com/earlyreaders

You'll get an email with a secret link to all the editable resources and templates. I'll also send you occasional writing and publishing resources, plus launch announcements for my books. You can unsubscribe anytime, keeping the resource pack.

As you read, look for this symbol:

It marks the start of a template you'll find in the resource pack. The end of each template is marked with a short line, like this:

―――

Ready to dive in? Keep reading to find out how alpha readers can supercharge your novel-writing process.

PART 1

ALPHA READERS

HOW NOT TO FORM AN ALPHA READER GROUP

When I'd written a single chapter of my first novel, I decided I wanted feedback on my rough draft as I wrote it. I Googled and discovered some authors use alpha readers before beta readers.

Alpha readers, I thought. *Yep, that's what I need.*

I spend too much time on social media, so I figured I'd use it to my advantage. I started a group on Facebook for my alpha readers. I invited my sister, my mom, and two book-loving friends to join. They all said yes.

Score! This writing thing was looking pretty great already. With a flourish, I set my rose-colored glasses on my nose.

The future was clear: I'd send my alpha readers my first chapter. They'd be so eager for more that they'd picket in front of my house, chanting, "FINISH THE BOOK! FINISH THE BOOK!" Then they'd return home to read my next chapter and give feedback. I'd graciously accept their feedback and write the best fantasy novel ever.

I uploaded my Word document into the Facebook group. All four of my readers gave me feedback. High on excitement, I published a post to my personal Facebook timeline about how I'd be happy to invite anyone to my alpha reader group for my new fantasy novel. Forty or fifty people volunteered. *Wow!* I added them to the group and kept writing.

And it fell apart. In fact, it fell apart in so many ways, I need bullet points to explain The Spectacular Downfall of My First Alpha Reader Group.

- Reading a **rough draft of a book one chapter at a time** is *not fun, y'all* . . .
- . . . especially when those chapters are in **Microsoft Word**, and it feels like work to read them . . .
- . . . and especially when the author is brand new and **doesn't know much about structuring a story**.
- A lot of the people who signed up as alpha readers **weren't readers in my genre**. They were excited for me, but once they read a bit of my odd little story about teenagers with magic, they weren't hooked.
- I had a group with a bunch of people who weren't participating, and Facebook doesn't much like that. Most of my posts ("Hey, everybody, I finished Chapter 18! I'd love your feedback!") got **swallowed into the bowels of Facebook's algorithms**.

I continued drafting that first book and, at some point, quietly stopped posting in my failed alpha reader group. Instead, I emailed chapters to my most loyal alpha readers.

We limped along, me trying to learn to write and them (sometimes) giving feedback. By the time I finished that first book, my sister and mom were the only alpha readers who completed it.

I'd learned a lot about writing along the way. I'd also learned a lot about how *not* to run an alpha reader group.

My mom and sister remained my loyal alpha readers for the second and third books in my trilogy. I also got feedback from my YA-reading kids.

I released all three books in quick succession and started work on a novella. By then, I had a small group of fans who'd read and enjoyed my completed series. My email list was growing. Best of all, I had a list of beta readers who'd given feedback on the trilogy.

I decided to start over with a new Facebook group for alpha readers. This time, I got it right. I invited existing fans into my group. I gave them much larger chunks of the book at a time, in formats that were easy to read. I provided clear guidelines on what kind of feedback I needed.

And it worked.

My alpha readers gave me quality feedback on that book . . . and they've done the same for every novel I've written since.

Ready to start your own alpha reader group? The following pages will guide you through the process, helping you avoid the pitfalls that waylaid me.

ALPHA READER OVERVIEW

Alpha readers focus on **big-picture feedback**. They catch *big, nasty worms* in areas like plot, characters, and pacing.

Many authors have never used alpha readers, so why should you consider it?

If you've ever sanded down a rough piece of wood, you may have used various types of sandpaper: coarse-grit to eliminate the biggest rough edges, medium-grit for lingering sharp spots, and fine-grit for final polishing.

Your alpha readers are coarse-grit sandpaper, helping you smooth out the roughest parts of your manuscript. Many authors go straight to beta readers, but that strategy turns betas into coarse sandpaper. In correcting the big stuff, they may miss the small stuff.

When you use alphas first, your betas become your mid-grit sandpaper. They catch the errors and weaknesses left over after the alpha round. Then you can utilize proofreaders and ARC readers as fine-grit sandpaper, so that your final work is truly polished.

As I mentioned in the last section, **I organize my alpha team within a Facebook group**. If you prefer not to use Facebook for this phase, **consider these alternate options:**

- **Google Docs**, which allows all your alpha readers to see each others' comments and respond to each other.
- **Discord**, a messaging/discussion app.
- **A private blog** (using the comments section to discuss feedback).
- **Email communications**, like you'll utilize during your beta phase. (We'll get into beta reading details in Part 2.)

If you choose an option other than Facebook, you can modify the advice in this book to work within that system.

Before moving on, take a bit of time to consider how big you'd like your alpha reader group to be. I suggest choosing **four to sixteen people**, depending how much feedback you want and how many people you feel comfortable sharing your words with.

Alpha reading is a real commitment and won't end up being a good fit for everyone. Assuming half your initial group of readers follow through, you can expect feedback from two to eight people.

In Summary: Alpha readers catch many of the big worms in your manuscript so that beta readers can help you refine it further. While I suggest hosting your alpha team on Facebook, there are other options. Decide how many alpha readers you want on your team, from four to sixteen.

Let's jump into the details of the alpha phase, starting with where to find readers.

If you're **just starting out as an author**, or you're published but **don't yet have fans or a way to contact your fans**, the next section ("Where to Find Alpha Readers If You Don't Have a Fan Base," p. 19) is for you.

On the other hand, if you're a **published author with a few (or more) fans**, and you have **at least one way to connect with those fans** (such as a newsletter and/or Facebook page or group), skip ahead to "Where to Find Alpha Readers If You Have a Fan Base" (p. 22).

WHERE TO FIND ALPHA READERS IF YOU DON'T HAVE A FAN BASE

If you're an author without a fan base, let me tell you something important. Come close. Are you listening?

You rock.

Seriously. Not only are you writing (or planning to write) a story that will transport people into the world of your imagination, you're also reading this book, which tells me you're striving for excellence.

Right now, it probably feels weird to think of having "fans." You're just a normal person. But when you work to make your book the best it can be, I bet you'll deserve fans. In fact, **alpha readers can help you write a book that's worthy of fans.**

Before those fans have found you, however, getting early readers can be challenging. Many authors will tell you, "Don't use friends and family as early readers. They probably don't read your genre and may not give you honest critiques." I have one big problem with this advice. When you're new at this novel-writing thing, you know what you've got?

Friends and family.

My first rule for finding alpha readers when you don't have fans is this:

Start with what you've got.

Think of the people you already know, in person and online. Ask yourself these questions:

- Who loves to read?
- Who enjoys my genre?
- Who might have a good, critical eye?
- Who do I trust?

You should always choose trustworthy alpha readers, but they don't have to tick all three of the other boxes. For instance, my mom doesn't generally read my genre (fantasy). But she loves to read, has a good eye for details, and is trustworthy. She was an alpha reader for my first series, and I appreciated her feedback and support.

As a beginning author, you're not looking for ideal alpha readers who'll be there for you twenty years from now. You're looking for people who will give you useful feedback as you write *one book* (or series). Some of them may "stick" and remain in your alpha reader group for years. Others may not work out, even for the first book. That's okay.

A word of caution: it's true that friends and family may not give you honest feedback. People you're close to may only want to tell you how awesome you are. It can be hard for them to read your words with a critical eye. Prepare yourself to remind them repeatedly—to beg them, if necessary—to critique your work. You need them to catch your worms.

If you've gotten to know other authors on social media or in offline writing groups, some of them may make great alpha readers. However, I don't suggest *only* having authors on your team, for reasons we'll discuss soon. So if you're lucky enough to be connected with other authors, consider them for your team *along with* your friends and family who love to read.

Once you have a list of people who might make decent alpha readers, invite them to join you. I'll get into more detail about how to ask them later.

You might be thinking, *Well, I'm connected with a bunch of people on [insert social media outlet]. Why don't I just post, asking who wants to be an alpha reader?*

As I said at the beginning of Part 1, I've tried that. You're likely to find better alpha readers if you screen them first by asking yourself the four questions I listed in the bullet points above. Early drafts are delicate, flawed things. You may not want to share your rough draft with your second cousin's neighbor who somehow convinced you to approve their friend request. Choose alpha readers you can trust.

In Summary: If you don't yet have a fan base, choose your alpha readers from trustworthy friends and family who love to read and will give you honest feedback. You can also consider adding fellow authors, if you know any.

The next section is for authors who already have a fan base. If that doesn't apply to you, feel free to skip ahead to the section titled, "Pros and Cons of Asking Fellow Authors to Be Early Readers" (p. 25).

WHERE TO FIND ALPHA READERS IF YOU HAVE A FAN BASE

If you have fans (even a few), take a minute to bask in your awesomeness.

Writing can be hard. Marketing can be even harder. Yet you've published something that real people . . . even a few . . . have read and enjoyed. Congratulations on writing stories that connect with readers!

Your first step in building an alpha reader group is to **choose potential members from your existing readers.** Consider these types of fans:

- **Beta readers:** If you've used betas in the past, were any of them particularly helpful, especially with big-picture feedback (on plot, characters, etc.)? If so, they might make great alpha readers.
- **Super fans:** Have you made special connections with any of your fans? Maybe Javier responds to all your author emails and gushes about your work, and Emma shares all your Facebook marketing posts. Fans who

love your work will often be thrilled when you ask them for feedback.
- **Close friends and family who love your writing and your genre:** You want to trust your alpha readers, so it's natural to ask friends and family. However, only choose those who will be willing to catch your worms (honestly critique your work), not just tell you how awesome you are.
- **General fans:** If you can't find enough alpha readers from those three groups, it's time to cast a wider net. You may choose to post on Facebook (on your author Page or Group), on other social media (if you connect with readers there), and/or in your author newsletter. Make it clear that you have a limited number of spots. That way you can be selective. You may even want to use an application, similar to the one I suggest using in the beta phase. (Check out "Pre-Beta Step 3: Create an Application," p. 80, if you want more details on this strategy.)

You can also consider **fellow authors who aren't your fans but understand your genre**.

Do you have your list of potential alpha readers? Before you reach out to any of them, ask yourself these questions:

- Is this person likely to give me useful, genre-specific feedback?
- Do I trust this person?

Make sure you can answer *yes* to both questions before inviting someone onto your alpha reader team.

In Summary: If you have fans, consider those who are most trustworthy and enthusiastic for your alpha team. You may

also want to add some fellow authors to your team.

In the next section, I'll help you think through the role fellow authors might play on your early reader teams.

PROS AND CONS OF ASKING FELLOW AUTHORS TO BE EARLY READERS

Many authors trade alpha and beta reading services with fellow authors. Let's discuss some of the pros and cons of such a strategy.

Pros:

- Other authors sometimes understand the **technical aspects** of writing. (While a non-author can say, "This chapter was slow" or "This sentence sounds wrong," an author may say, "Your first plot point should happen earlier" or "You switched tenses here.")
- If you trade with other authors, they'll hopefully **follow through** since they want you to do the same for them.

Cons:

- Trades can end up feeling **obligatory**, taking the fun out of alpha and beta reading.
- With a trade, one author may **resent** the other. One

manuscript may need more work than the other, or one author may give less detailed feedback than the other.
- When trading, sometimes authors may be **hesitant to be totally honest** if they don't like something, lest the other author gets hurt and no longer wants to trade.

If you trade alpha or beta reading services with other authors, I suggest you also bring in some team members who are *readers only*. They may give you different perspectives than fellow authors will.

Here's my policy for working with fellow authors on alpha, beta, and ARC reading:

I work on a pay-it-forward basis rather than a trade basis.

I offer to be an early reader, or agree to be one, *when I want to*. I might do it because a book sounds interesting or because I want to do a favor for another author. I don't expect the author I'm helping to return the favor.

Similarly, when another author acts as one of my early readers, I assume they want to be on my team. I don't automatically offer to read for them. (However, if they ask me to, there's a good chance I'll say yes.)

I don't track how many authors read for me and how many I read for. I just try to be generous while keeping healthy boundaries.

Paying it forward rather than trading is remarkably freeing for me. I give honest feedback to authors without worrying about what feedback they'll give me. I'm less likely to fight resentment, because if I said I'd be an early reader, it was because I wanted to. I give genuine appreciation to fellow authors who act as my early readers, because I know such a service is a true gift.

If you're concerned about the "cons" of trading early reading services with fellow authors, consider whether a pay-it-forward strategy might work better for you. If you implement this strategy (and are generous along the way), I hope you find it as satisfying as I do.

In Summary: Fellow authors often have great advice, but beware of the pitfalls of trading alpha and beta reading services with them. You may prefer a pay-it-forward mindset instead.

Now that you know where to find early readers, it's time for the next step: inviting them.

HOW TO INVITE SOMEONE TO BE AN ALPHA READER

Reach out to your potential alpha readers using whatever communication method you prefer—email, text, Facebook Messenger, etc. You can even call them if you're not afraid of phone calls like I am. (What can I say? I'm an introvert.)

Below, you'll find a sample message you can use to invite someone to join your alpha reader team.

In communication templates here and throughout the book, I've underlined the portions you'll need to modify. Where you'll need to add a link, I've reminded you {between curly brackets}. My notes to you are in [square brackets].

Remember, you can get these resources in editable formats as part of my resource pack. Just visit this link:

carolbethanderson.com/earlyreaders

Subject line [if using email]: Name, I'd love to invite you to my alpha reading team

Hi, Name,

I'm working on my next mystery novel, and I'm building a team of alpha readers—people who will read a very early version of my book, then give me feedback.

I'd love for you to join my team, because I think your suggestions will make my next book even better! I'm only asking a few people to join, and I think you'd be a great fit.

Let me tell you a little about how alpha reading works.

I'll add alpha readers to a small, select Facebook group. As I write, I'll share the manuscript with the group, and we'll discuss what's working and what isn't. Alpha readers don't need a sharp eye for grammar or other details. I'll want big-picture feedback on plot, characters, etc.

Alpha reading is a commitment, and I always want it to be a privilege, not an obligation. If you're interested in joining, I'll be thrilled to welcome you to the group. If you're not interested or don't have time, no hard feelings. Please let me know either way.

Thanks for your enthusiasm for my books!

-Author Name

If you've chosen a venue other than Facebook for your alpha team, simply edit the invitation to reflect that.

In Summary: Invite people to join your alpha team by sending them a low-pressure, enthusiastic message explaining the process.

Asking people to join your group is great . . . but they need a group to join. In the next section, we'll talk about forming your group.

HOW TO ORGANIZE YOUR ALPHA READER GROUP

I have several reasons for using **Facebook** to host my alpha reader group:

- It's **free**.
- Many people **already have Facebook accounts**.
- It's helpful to **discuss** big-picture topics like plot and characters within a group.
- You'll be giving your alpha readers chunks of a far-less-than-perfect manuscript. Let's be honest, it's not the most ideal way to read a book. The **community vibe** of a Facebook group encourages readers to engage with each other and with you. That may make them more likely to keep their commitment.

This section will go over the ins and outs of setting up an alpha reader group on Facebook. If you're hosting your alpha group elsewhere, you'll still find some suggestions that you can modify for the method you've chosen.

Let's get some preliminary stuff out of the way first. Whatever your feelings about Facebook, a whole lot of readers use it. If you don't yet have an author presence there, this is a great time to remedy that.

I suggest you create both **a Facebook author page and a reader group** before you create your alpha reader group. Here are a few tips:

- When you create your Facebook author page, choose the "Public Figure" page option. An author page is a great way for *anyone* to check out your work.
- Once you have a page, you can start a reader group, which is more personal. It's a place for your fans and supporters to gather and have real conversations with you.
- For reader group suggestions, check out the article "How to Create, Cultivate, & Maintain an Active Author/Reader Group on Facebook!" by Samantha A. Cole on her *One Author to Another* blog.

Got your author page and reader group? Excellent. It's time to set up your alpha reader group. Follow these steps:

- Choose whether to start a group using your **personal Facebook account or your author Page.** If you're unsure how to start the group, Google it. (It changes depending what device you're on, and Facebook frequently updates their interface.)
- Give your group a **simple name** (like Liz B. Author's Alpha Readers).
- Make it a **Private group**. (This prevents the world from seeing your work-in-progress. It also keeps your work

from being considered "published," which is important if you're querying agents and/or publishers.)
- It's fun to have a **cover photo,** but it's not required. (You can find images that are free for commercial use on Pexels or Pixabay. Another great resource is Canva, an online, free image editor that makes it easy to create a Facebook cover photo.)
- In your group's Settings, you can **customize the group's URL** (such as www.facebook.com/groups/lizbauthoralpha).
- Also in Settings, ensure that **only admins and moderators can approve members**.
- Create a **Group Description** in Settings. I suggest something along these lines:

This is a group for Author Name's alpha readers. While this is an invitation-only group, feel free to request membership in Author First Name's reader group. Search Facebook for "My Amazing Reader Group."

- To help you screen potential group members, Facebook allows you to add **Membership Questions**. I suggest adding the following question:

Membership in this group is by invitation only. Did Author Name invite you to join? (By the way, you're welcome to join My Amazing Reader Group!)

[Create two multiple-choice answers:]

- Yes, Author First Name invited me to join.
- No, I'll join My Amazing Reader Group instead.

Now that you've started a group, send the URL to those who've agreed to join. Then **create a welcome post** that sets clear expectations for your alpha readers. (If you're not using Facebook, you can welcome your team through an email, a Discord message, etc.) Here's a sample welcome message:

Welcome to my alpha reader group! I chose each of you to join because I'm confident your feedback will be truly helpful to me. I appreciate you.

Here's how this group will work:

Each time I finish a quarter of my manuscript, I'll post a download link. I'll tag each of you in a comment to make sure you see the post.

The sooner you can read and give feedback, the better . . . but I know how busy life can be, and this is a guilt-free group. I'll appreciate your feedback whenever you provide it.

Here are some simple feedback guidelines:

- I'm not looking for grammar and typo corrections. Those will come later.
- I'm looking for big-picture feedback on topics such as plot, characters, and pacing. I want to hear what you loved, what you hated, and what confused you.

When you post, please start by telling me which book you're giving feedback on and what portion of the book. Also, please use a line of dots to make sure other group members don't see any spoilers. It should look like this:

Book Title, Quarter 1:

.

.

.

.

.

.

.

I just finished this section, and here's my feedback! I loved how the unicorn ate the dragon. But it didn't make sense that the time machine exploded! I also thought...

You get the idea.

I want this group to be interactive, so please comment on each other's posts. And I'm sure it goes without saying, but please always be respectful to me and the others in the group. Be honest and be kind.

Thanks for helping make my novel the best it can be!

After publishing this post, **pin it to the top of your group**. Here are instructions on how to do that if you're on the desktop browser version of Facebook:

- Click the three dots at the top right of the post. Click "Mark as Announcement."
- Reload your post by clicking the time and date at the top of it.
- Click the three dots again, and click "Pin to top."

In Summary: If you choose to run your alpha team through Facebook, take a little time to set up the group properly. No matter how you organize your team, be sure to welcome every member and tell them what to expect during the process.

If you finished all the steps up to this point, congratulations! You've got an alpha reader group. Next, let's talk about when to ask for their feedback.

HOW OFTEN TO REQUEST FEEDBACK FROM ALPHA READERS

If you're writing a full-length novel, **I suggest providing one-quarter of your book at a time to your alpha readers.**

Allowing group members to read your rough manuscript . . . your book baby . . . might be scary. Keep in mind that you invited these readers to join your team because you trust them. It may even help to tell your group how nervous this makes you. I bet they'll encourage you to share, no matter how imperfect your rough draft is.

There are two main reasons to provide your manuscript to alpha readers one-quarter at a time.

- Your readers get long enough chunks of the book to really **get invested**.
- If you use basic story-structure guidelines, **you'll already be writing your novel in four parts.**

Wait a minute, you may be thinking. *I thought novels had three acts.*

Well, yes. And no. Many authors write using a three-act plot structure. However, in the traditional three-act structure, Act Two is twice as long as either of the other acts . . . and it's split in half by a big scene at the midpoint. Some authors and story-structure experts use the terminology "four acts" instead of "three acts." They're just splitting up that long second act into two parts.

In a novel written using traditional story structure, your **first plot point, midpoint/second plot point, and third plot point** are natural places to split up your manuscript for alpha readers.

I can already hear the frustrated cries coming from some of you: "But I'm a pantser, not a plotter!"

Let me reassure you, I'm not anti-pantser. (A pantser "flies by the seat of their pants" when writing a novel, whereas a plotter outlines a novel in advance.)

Effective pantsers often write using story-structure guidelines without planning it in advance, thanks to their great instincts. If you're a pantser, you can guesstimate when you've hit the end of each quarter of your book. Better yet, do a bit of reading on story structure so you recognize when your brilliant mind is naturally hitting those important, end-of-quarter plot points.

If you'd like to read up on the principles of story structure, check out "Appendix 1: Story Structure Resources" (p. 213), which lists various resources, including a free blog series on the topic.

Not every great novel fits into traditional story-structure guidelines. Literary fiction in particular tends to chart its own course. If you're writing in a style that doesn't fit these guidelines, you can split up your work in other ways. Maybe you have a sense of how long it will be, and you can estimate when you've reached the end of a quarter. Or you can simply break it up after significant plot events.

While I love getting feedback as I draft, that won't work for every author.

Some authors like to write the entire book before anyone else gets their eyes on it. Other authors write out of sequence, and alpha readers probably don't want to read a book that way.

If providing portions of your book to alpha readers while you're drafting doesn't work for you, no problem. You can follow the instructions in this section but provide your group with the entire book all at once, instead of sending it in pieces. You can still discuss their feedback within the Facebook group (or using whatever other platform you've chosen).

In Summary: I suggest sending a full-length novel to your alpha readers approximately one-quarter at a time.

Once you've written the first quarter of your book, congratulations! You're almost ready for feedback from your alpha readers. First, let's address a practical consideration: what format(s) will you use for your manuscript?

FORMATTING A MANUSCRIPT FOR YOUR EARLY READERS

When I was writing my first series, I shared Microsoft Word documents with my alpha readers. Unfortunately, some early readers would rather not open up a .docx file. Why?

Reading a Word document feels like work, not leisure.

There's already a certain element of *work* involved for alpha and beta readers. They're expected to think critically as they read and to take time to share their thoughts. However, reading should be fun too. That's why now, **I provide manuscripts to my early readers in three mobile-friendly digital formats:**

- **mobi** (for Kindle and Kindle apps)
- **ePub** (for other e-readers and apps)
- **PDF** (for almost any device)

Mobile-friendly formats allow early readers to take a phone, tablet, or e-reader to bed with them and dive into your story. (If they're using a mobi or ePub, they can even easily take notes as they read.) I want my early readers to look forward to getting lost in my words, rather than thinking, "Ugh, one more task in front of the computer."

If you've never generated mobi, ePub, and PDF files, no problem. Here are some resources for you to check out:

- **Reedsy** offers a free online book writing/formatting tool where you can draft your book (or import your Word file) and export to mobi, ePub, and print-ready PDF formats.
- **Draft2Digital** is an ebook distribution platform that allows you to upload Word documents and export them to mobi, ePub, and print-ready PDF formats.
- **KDP** (Kindle Digital Publishing) is the website self-publishers use to publish directly to Amazon. As part of your Kindle ebook creation process, you can upload a Microsoft Word doc, then export as mobi and HTML files by clicking "Preview on your computer." You can then use a free converter like Convert.io to make an ePub file. You'll need to use the "Save As" command in Word to generate a PDF.
- **Calibre** is free, open-source software that you can use to generate mobi and ePub files. You'll need to use the "Save As" command in Word to generate a PDF.
- **Scrivener** is software used to organize and write books. You can use it to generate mobi, ePub, and print-ready PDF files.
- **Atticus** is software arriving in 2021 that works on Mac, Windows, Linux, and Chromebook. It generates ePub and print-ready PDF files from Microsoft Word files. You can then use a free converter like Convert.io to make a mobi file (to distribute directly to your early readers). You also have the option of drafting your book within Atticus.

- **Vellum** is Mac-only software that generates mobi, ePub, and print-ready PDF files from Microsoft Word files.

Want more details on all these options? Consult "Appendix 2: File Formatting Options" (p. 215) for a detailed breakdown of the pros and cons of each formatting option, along with extra notes and tips to help you format successfully.

If you've never formatted books before, I suggest starting with Reedsy or, if you're a self-publishing Mac user and want a more flexible, robust option, Vellum. Note that while Reedsy is free, Vellum is quite pricey.

After reading all that, you may be asking, *Can't I just send them my book in Word or Google Docs format?*

Of course you can. However, you may have happier readers if you take the time to provide them with other formats. And happier readers are more likely to follow through.

One more note: When I format my book one-quarter at a time for my alpha readers, I always include the previous quarter(s) too. In other words, a "Quarter 3" manuscript contains Quarters 1, 2, and 3. Sometimes readers want to look back at previous chapters.

In Summary: To make the early reading process more enjoyable for your readers, consider formatting your manuscript into mobile-friendly file types (mobi, ePub, and PDF). Reedsy offers a good, free formatting program, but there are several other excellent options.

Once you've chosen a formatting option, you'll need to decide how to distribute the files to your readers. We'll discuss your options in the next section.

PROVIDING BOOK FILES TO READERS

If you choose to provide your readers with mobi, ePub, and PDF files, **you'll need a good way for them to download your book**. Thankfully, there are multiple websites designed to make this easy on you and your readers.

Here are three such sites for you to check out.

- **StoryOrigin:** Upload as a Reader Magnet if you want to capture your readers' email addresses. If you don't need their email addresses, upload as a Direct Download. **Free and paid membership options.**
- **ProlificWorks:** Upload as a New Book, then create a Giveaway. If you want to capture readers' email addresses, you'll need a paid account. **Free and paid membership options.**
- **BookFunnel:** Set up a Landing Page for your book, and choose whether to require an email address. BookFunnel offers watermarked files in some of its plans, which

helps protect your work from pirates. **Price: Paid membership options only.**

All these sites also offer plenty of ways for self-publishing authors to partner with other authors to market their books and build their email-subscriber lists.

Some authors send manuscript files directly to their early readers via email. If your early readers are tech savvy enough to transfer these files to their devices, that's a good option. (The sites listed above make this transfer process easier on readers.)

In Summary: Multiple websites make it easy to share formatted book files with readers.

Once you've set up the first quarter of your book on one of the sites above, it'll be time to share it with your readers and ask for their feedback. The next section will guide you through that process.

REQUESTING FEEDBACK FROM ALPHA READERS

It's time to ask your alpha readers what they think of your story. *How* you ask for feedback is vitally important. That's a rule I'm still learning.

Recently I walked up to my husband and asked, "So . . . what do you think?"

He tilted his head to the side, eyes on my hair. "You got your hair cut? It doesn't look that different."

I rolled my eyes. "I didn't get a haircut. I got new glasses!"

In my husband's defense, I didn't get the feedback I wanted because my request was unclear. I'd talked recently about getting a haircut, and he assumed that's what I was asking about.

(And in my defense, my new glasses were *really cute*. Of course I thought he'd notice them!)

As authors, when we don't get the feedback we want on our manuscripts, it's often because we're unclear in our requests. So let's discuss *the big ask* (for feedback).

You've got one-quarter of a manuscript. You've formatted it and uploaded it to a distribution site.

Requesting feedback may excite you . . . or it may terrify you. If you're like me, both are true. I get excited to hear what real readers think of my work. But there's always that little question . . .

What if they hate it?

We'll address this fear in more detail later in the book, but here's something I like to remind myself of:

If my book sucks, I'd rather hear it from early readers than from public reviewers.

Whether you're excited or scared, when it's time for feedback, start a new post in your alpha reader group (or share in whatever way is appropriate if you're not using Facebook). If you have a book cover and don't mind sharing it, add it to your post. (It catches the eye and makes it easier for your readers to go back and find the post later.)

Here's a sample post:

Hi, alpha readers. I'm excited to share Quarter <u>2</u> of <u>*The Greatest Novel Ever*</u> with you!

You can download it at {link}. You'll be able to read it on your Kindle or other e-reader, or on your computer if you download the PDF file. Please let me know if you have any trouble getting the file onto your device.

[Include this paragraph if sharing quarters two through four.] This quarter starts with Chapter <u>12</u>.

As a reminder, here are feedback guidelines:

-I'm **not looking for grammar and typo corrections**. Those will come later.

-I'm looking for **big-picture feedback on topics such as plot, characters, and pacing**. I want to hear what you loved, what you hated, and what confused you.

<u>In this paragraph, tell your readers anything in particular you want them to look for. For instance, "I'd like to know how you feel about the first scene," or "Please tell me any predictions you have about who the murderer is!"</u>

When you're ready to give feedback, please start a post in the group so others can comment on it. Check out the pinned post at the top of the group if you need a reminder on how to format your feedback post.

The sooner you can give feedback, the better, but I know you have other responsibilities, and I'll always respect your time. [If sharing the **final** quarter of the book, include the next sentence.] **I'd love to hear from you by <u>January 20</u>** so I can use your feedback in my first big round of revisions.

Thank you so much in advance for reading and giving your honest opinions.

One more note: **if you're using the ePub or mobi (Kindle) version of the book**, you can take notes as you read, then export them and copy/paste them into your feedback post. The process on ePub varies depending on what app or device you're using. If you're using a Kindle, please read this document BEFORE downloading your book file, to make sure you're able to export your notes:

carolbethanderson.com/how-to-take-and-export-kindle-notes/

———

Publish the post. Mark it as an Announcement. Then post a comment tagging every group member, to ensure they see the post.

The final link in that post leads to an article on my website for Kindle readers who want to take notes on their Kindle device and share those notes. (Unfortunately, the process for doing that isn't very intuitive.) Feel free to share the link with your readers, or copy and paste the article onto your own website so you can send them to your site instead of mine.

In Summary: To get usable feedback from your alpha readers, be specific in what you ask for.

You've taken the first step by asking for feedback. Your job isn't done, though. Next, we'll discuss other steps you can take to keep your alpha readers engaged.

HOW TO ENCOURAGE ALPHA READER FOLLOW-THROUGH

Not every alpha reader is likely to follow through. That's okay. Sometimes alpha readers sign up, then realize it's not a good fit. If half your alpha readers follow through, that's just fine.

However, there are some steps you can take to encourage readers who *are* "good fits" to follow-through.

Write a good book. This one sounds obvious, right? But as authors, we know it's a lot harder than it sounds. Here are some tips to help you write a book your alpha readers will be excited to dig into.

- **Read books and articles on the craft of writing** (such as the story structure resources listed in Appendix 1, p. 213).
- **Read lots of novels in your genre.** It's incredibly important to "soak up" the types of stories you want to sell.
- **Consider reading through your manuscript once** (making some edits along the way) before sending it to

alpha readers. I do this a chapter at a time—draft, read through/light edit, move on. You may prefer another process, such as writing the whole quarter, then reading it. I'll admit, this goes against a lot of drafting advice, which says to keep writing without editing. That's valid too. However, I want my alpha readers to enjoy reading something that's a little less rough than a standard rough draft.

Give your readers status updates. Every so often, write a post in the group, letting your alpha readers know how things are going and when they can expect the next quarter of your book.

Give your readers "inside information." Recently, I posted in my group, telling my alpha readers which scenes were making me cry as I revised. If you're researching an interesting topic as you write, you can share cool facts or resources. Your group should be a fun place for your readers to hang out. Make your alpha readers feel like insiders.

Ask your alpha readers for status updates. If you haven't gotten the feedback you're looking for, write a post kindly asking your readers to update you on when they'll have feedback for you. It may light a fire under them.

Ask your alpha readers for advice and ideas as you write. Sometimes I'm stuck on something, and I go to my alpha readers for advice. They love giving input. In one of my fantasy series, the characters discover a subway system in an ancient city. I'd called it an *Undertrain*, but then I realized another author's series used the same terminology. I asked my alpha readers to help me come up with a new name for the subway. (It's now the *Extrain*.)

In Summary: You can improve alpha reader follow-through by focusing on the craft of writing and by engaging often with your alpha team.

As your readers dig into your book and you keep in touch with them, they'll start telling you what they think . . . and you'll need to respond appropriately. I'll give tips on how to do that next.

RESPONDING TO FEEDBACK

One of my alpha readers recently posted in my group, saying, "I read the third quarter in one day!" I loved getting her enthusiastic feedback.

Yet I still haven't forgotten the feedback I got from alpha readers when I posted the first quarter of Book 2 of my series. "I liked this character in Book 1," they told me, "but he seems like a jerk now." That type of critique never feels great (even if it's true . . . which, in this case, it was. They'd caught a big, juicy worm.)

Two alpha readers, two very different posts. Yet I started my responses to both of them in the same way: I thanked them.

Your first response to honest, non-abusive feedback should always be gratitude.

Also consider these tips as you draft your response to feedback:

- **Be specific.** Tell your alpha reader what particular feedback you found most useful. Praise them for their insight.

- **Have a real conversation.** Ask for clarification on points you're not clear on. Explain more of your thinking to your reader. Build a relationship. (Facebook makes this easy.)
- **Consider telling your readers why you're not taking certain advice.** Be careful—it's easy to muck this up if you're defensive. (I remember an alpha reader telling me she wanted more worldbuilding depth in a novella. I explained that novellas are too short to go into that much depth. Later, I had to eat my words when I realized she was right. That novella needed to be a novel, and eventually, it turned into one.) If you can avoid defensiveness, your readers may appreciate a brief, friendly explanation of why you're not following their advice, or why you're only following part of it.
- If you aren't sure which feedback you'll use, simply **thank your reader for giving you something new to consider**.

Negative feedback can be hard to take. If it makes you want to crawl into a hole and never visit your alpha reader group again, let me assure you that you're not alone.

Should you respond to constructive criticism? Yes. But when critiques hurt, you may need to take a break first. Talk to a friend or therapist; get some sunshine; cuddle with a pet; read a great book; take a bath—whatever you need to do to get your mind into a better place. If this is a big struggle for you, I have more tips in the section titled, "How Do I Get Over My Fear of Feedback?" in the Q&A near the end of the book (p. 201).

In Summary: Thank your alpha readers for feedback; tell them which critiques helped the most; and have real conversations with them about their advice.

We need to show appreciation to our readers, whether we're utilizing their feedback or not. But how do we decide which feedback to take and which to toss? We'll address that in the next section.

DECIDING WHICH FEEDBACK TO UTILIZE WHEN REVISING

If you have enough early readers, you'll get contradictory feedback from them. You've got a group made up of real people with diverse opinions. That's a good thing.

But it can be confusing and stressful. You may look at all the varied opinions and feel that in asking for so many opinions, you've created a monster.

To be honest, I regularly get overwhelmed by feedback. So let's both take a deep breath. We've got this.

Here's how I determine whether to change my manuscript based on an alpha or beta reader's opinion:

- If the feedback **feels right in my gut, I change it**, even if only one person brought it up.
- If I don't automatically agree with the feedback but **more than one person brings it up, I *consider* changing it**.
- Sometimes, even when multiple people don't like a

decision I made, I **stick to my guns** because I feel it's the **right direction** for my book to take. That being said, it's easy to fall back on "artistic integrity" because it's hard to take critiques. If that describes you, I encourage you to try making some changes, even ones you aren't sure about. You can always go back to your original plan if the changes don't work.

Often, readers give me feedback that's solid at its roots, but their suggestion for fixing it doesn't feel right. For example, a reader told me she thought a breakup happened suddenly and should perhaps be pushed farther back in the book. I had reasons for keeping the timing as it was, so instead of moving the event, I justified it through foreshadowing in previous scenes. It's important to **consider the critique behind the feedback even if you don't like your reader's suggestion for fixing it**.

In Summary: When considering whether to utilize feedback, consider your own "gut feelings," how many people gave you a critique, and what your vision for your book is.

Your revisions will be easier if you organize the feedback you receive. Keep reading for tips on how to do that.

HOW TO ORGANIZE FEEDBACK

When my alpha reading round comes to a close, my Facebook group is full of feedback to process. It can be truly overwhelming. I have to organize the feedback to make it more manageable before I start my big revisions.

I'll tell you my organization process, but yours may differ. Like so many aspects of writing, this is all about figuring out what works for you.

I organize feedback in Microsoft Word. I often copy/paste my readers' words directly, but sometimes I summarize the changes that need to be made (especially if the feedback was long or particularly hard to take.)

In my feedback document, I have sections for overall feedback, each quarter's feedback, and each chapter's feedback. It looks something like this:

> **Overall**
> *Could you put in more physical descriptions of the characters?*

Quarter 1
This quarter felt a little slow. Maybe more explosions? Introduce the love interest sooner.

Chapter 1
I loved the first sentence! Hooked me right away.

Chapter 2
You mentioned it was about to rain, but then you said the sun was shining.

As you can see, I like to paste in some positive feedback as well as criticism. That's because critiques can be discouraging, and I want to remember that my readers are enjoying parts of my book too.

If you get a lot of feedback, the document where you compile it may get long. Microsoft Word has a tool called a Navigation Pane. It allows you to create a clickable outline so you can easily navigate from one part of your document to another. For a short video tutorial on this feature, check out my blog post called "Organizing Alpha and Beta Reader Feedback" at carolbethanderson.com.

Here are two more tips to help you organize your feedback:

- **Make a separate list of the top issues you need to remember throughout your book.** These might be issues like, "More physical descriptions of characters" or "Remember John has an injured left arm." I like to handwrite this list with pretty pens and keep it next to my keyboard. That way I can review it every time I sit down to revise. A fellow author, Yvette Bostic, told me she puts her "big points" on sticky notes and posts them around her computer.

- **Strikethrough each piece of feedback when you've incorporated it into your revisions.** In Word, highlight the feedback, then click Command Shift X (Mac) or Ctrl Shift X (PC) to strikethrough. It helps you easily see what pieces of feedback you haven't used yet. Plus, it's satisfying.

In Summary: By organizing your early reader feedback, you'll make your life easier when it's time to revise.

When you reach the point where you're organizing feedback for all four quarters of your book, you're nearly done with the alpha phase . . . hopefully. In the next section, we'll discuss what to consider when you're thinking about wrapping up this phase.

HOW TO KNOW WHEN THE ALPHA READER PHASE IS COMPLETE

I love when my writing process is simple. Early draft/alpha readers, revisions, beta readers, more revisions, done.

With some books, however, it's not that easy.

When I get feedback from alpha readers that leads me to make *big* plot changes, sometimes I do a second round of alpha reading for anyone who wants to participate.

Other times, alpha feedback leads me to make major changes to Quarter 1, 2, or 3 *before* I move on with drafting. In that case, I provide a new version of the partial manuscript to any alphas who want to read it. Some readers prefer to read only the parts I changed, so I tell them what chapters I made major revisions to.

When do I feel comfortable no longer asking for alpha feedback? **When my characters and plot are solid and headed in the right direction.** If I'm going to add a major character or change big plot points, I usually ask my alpha readers for feedback on those edits.

Once I've got that solid draft, the alpha phase is officially over. However, as I do pre-beta revisions, I often run smaller changes past the group. I don't expect them all to give feedback, but some of them love doing so. For example, I recently rewrote the epilogue to a novel. I posted screenshots of the new epilogue in my alpha group and got some quick feedback from my readers. In the comments, I went back and forth with them, trying to get the final lines just right.

If you'd like to go into more depth on the steps between your rough draft and final draft, Appendix 3 (p. 221) gives you a sample early reading, revision, and editing process.

In Summary: If you make big changes to your plot or characters, you'll probably want to get your alpha readers' feedback on those. Your alpha phase is complete when your characters and plot are solid and headed in the right direction.

Your alpha reader *group* doesn't need to end just because your alpha *phase* ended for one particular book. A great alpha group can help you from one book to the next. Along the way, you may at times need to remove members. Let's cover when and how to do that.

REMOVING INACTIVE GROUP MEMBERS

As I've mentioned, some alpha readers won't be able to follow through. It's always a good idea to reach out to inactive members to see if they plan to become active. If they need to take a bit of time off but they plan to come back for your next book, consider letting them stay in the group.

However, **if alpha reading wasn't a good fit** (because they got busy, lost interest, etc.), **it's time to respectfully remove them from the group.**

For a long time, I had a hard time with this. I didn't want members to feel rejected or uncomfortable. However, I also didn't like offering spoilers to readers who couldn't participate by giving critiques. And I had good reason to believe my inactive members wouldn't turn active any time soon.

Knowing I needed to write this very section of this very book, I recently removed members from my group.

And . . . dare I say it? It was easy.

I didn't just boot them out, though. I sent them each a private message to explain why I was removing them. It went something like this:

Hi, Name! I'm doing some maintenance on my alpha reader group. Thank you for your willingness to join the group. I know that due to time constraints or other considerations, it's not working out for you to alpha read. I'll go ahead and remove you from the group, but if you ever decide you want to return, just let me know. Thanks again!

If you're considering removing someone from your group for a reason besides inactivity, check out the section titled "When Is It Time to 'Fire Someone' from an Early Reader Team?" in the Questions & Answers at the back of the book (p. 195).

In Summary: If someone isn't active in your alpha group, you can remove them. Be sure to give them a polite, upbeat explanation.

Shrinking your group isn't fun. Thankfully, you have the power to grow your group too. We'll discuss when and how to do that in the next section.

ADDING NEW GROUP MEMBERS

You may occasionally want to **add new group members** for any of these reasons:

- You've **lost group members**.
- You'd like **more feedback** than you're getting.
- You're **shifting genres** and need alpha readers who fit your new genre better. (In this case, you may choose to start an entirely new group.)
- A **beta reader gives you great, big-picture feedback**, and you think they'd make a great alpha reader.

Invite them to join, as we discussed in "How to Invite Someone to Be an Alpha Reader" (p. 28). Tag any new group member(s) in your group's introductory/how-to post, or send them a link to it, so they understand how to give feedback. You can also introduce them to the group in a welcome post.

In Summary: When you want more feedback, you can welcome new members to your existing alpha group.

Congratulations! You've got the tools you need to form and run an alpha reader group. However, before we wrap up this part of the book, let's talk about avoiding a trap many of us fall into when we're drafting.

DON'T GET LOST IN YOUR DRAFTING CAVE

As I write my first draft, **it's easy to get lost in a drafting cave, where there's nothing but me and the words.**

Anyone relate? It's part of the beauty of writing fiction, getting so wrapped up in our own stories that we don't want to think of anything else.

However, pretty soon, we'll need beta readers, then ARC readers. And eventually, we'll need *paying* readers. That means that your drafting phase should also be the start of your marketing phase. (And here's a pro tip: the marketing phase never ends.)

Below, I'll list **a few marketing activities** you can consider squeezing in, between writing all those amazing scenes. Because this isn't a book about marketing, I won't go into detail. But if you have questions about any of these topics, there are plenty of YouTube videos, blog posts, and books to guide you.

- **Social media (Facebook):** As I mentioned earlier, I suggest starting both a Facebook page and a reader

group for your fans (even if that's just friends and family who think it's cool you're writing a book). (See the article "How to Create, Cultivate, & Maintain an Active Author/Reader Group on Facebook!" by Samantha A. Cole on her One Author to Another blog.)
- **Social media (other):** Now is a great time to start building a following on Instagram, Twitter, TikTok, or other social media sites. You don't need to be active on *every* site. Likely you'll have one or two social media sites that resonate with you. Focus on those.
- **Website:** Set up a website (even a simple, free one).
- **Newsletter:** Start a newsletter where you can update potential readers (probably friends and family at this point) on your progress. (I'll mention newsletters several times throughout this book. If you don't have one, I suggest you check out the article, "0 to 1,000+ mailing list subscribers" on the StoryOrigin blog.)
- **Education:** Educate yourself on publishing and marketing. Search for Facebook groups, books, and articles on these topics.

Why should you focus on all these activities now? Because once it's time to publish, you'll be completely overwhelmed if you're also trying to establish all your marketing. By putting a little time into these marketing activities *as you draft*, you'll be more prepared for the next steps in your publication process.

In Summary: While you're drafting your book, connect with others through social media, a website, and a newsletter. Also take the time to educate yourself on publishing and marketing.

Let's talk about how to make adjustments to the alpha reader phase so it works for you.

THE ALPHA READER PHASE: MAKE IT YOUR OWN

Don't want to send long messages to potential alpha readers? Feel a headache coming on when you read about ePubs and mobi files? I got you!

Here are some ideas to adjust *your* alpha reader group to fit *you*.

- Put **your own personality** into your communications with alpha readers. Maybe my templates are too wordy for you or include far too few swear words. *Hey, you do you.*
- Share **more or less than one-quarter of the book** at a time. (When I wrote a fairly short novella, I shared half the book at a time.)
- **Provide your manuscript in other formats.** My readers respond well to mobile-friendly formats, particularly mobi and ePub. However, yours may feel differently. Ask them how they'd like to read your book. Experiment with as many formats as you please.
- **You may choose not to have an alpha reader phase.**

Maybe you'll use critique partners instead. Do what works for you.

In Summary: The book you're writing is *yours*, and you can adjust the processes I've suggested to fit you.

Once you've utilized your alpha readers' feedback, it'll be time to hand off your manuscript to a new group: beta readers. Part 2 will help you create a truly helpful beta team.

PART 2
BETA READERS

BETA READER OVERVIEW

Early readers catch the worms—but alpha and beta readers catch different *types* of worms.

Alpha readers catch big, nasty worms. They help you avoid big-picture mistakes in areas like structure, characters, pacing, and plot.

A Facebook group works well in the alpha phase, because it's easy to share thoughts on a few big worms in one Facebook post. An alpha reader might use five paragraphs for all their feedback—on the character they're finding annoying, the fast pace they loved, and a few weaknesses in the plot.

Beta readers may still catch some big worms. (Your characters and plot won't be perfect at this phase.) **However, they also catch little worms**, like awkward phrasing and your tendency to start too many sentences with the word *But*. (That last example came from a certain author whose words you're reading now.)

With so many little worms to catch, some beta readers will go into lots of detail in their feedback. One of my beta readers is an expert at finding little worms, sometimes sending me several hundred notes for a book. That would be way too much for an alpha-style Facebook post.

Because I structure my beta phase differently from my alpha phase, beta readers can send me as much feedback as they want, in a format that works for them. We'll go into detail on how the beta phase works in the coming sections.

While I organize my alpha and beta teams differently, many other aspects of the two phases are similar. As we encounter those similarities in Part 2, I'll direct you back to the appropriate sections in Part 1, rather than repeating myself.

In Summary: Because beta readers often give more detailed feedback than alpha readers, I encourage you to organize your beta phase differently (not through a Facebook group).

Before you find beta readers, I suggest you take four preparatory steps. We'll discuss those next. And if checklists make you squirm, sit tight. I'm here to help make this process as painless as possible so you can get back to your muse.

PRE-BETA STEP 1: POLISH UP THAT MANUSCRIPT!

All early readers should expect some of those annoying imperfections we're calling *worms*. However, if you want happy beta readers, you need to **smash a whole lot of worms before you send them your book.**

As in the alpha phase, you should always focus on writing a good book by learning about the craft of writing and by reading plenty of books in your genre.

But unlike the alpha phase, you shouldn't send an early, messy draft to betas. Hopefully you've fixed all those big worms your alpha readers found, but you also need to do some small-worm hunting before sending your book to betas. Try to provide your betas with a book that's not crammed with grammatical errors and typos.

Your book doesn't need to be perfect, but betas are more likely to enjoy it and finish it if it's fairly polished. And when you catch a lot of your worms in advance, eagle-eyed beta readers are more likely to make an effort to find the remaining errors. If your manuscript has hundreds or thousands of errors, you can't expect betas to point them all out.

Here are a few **tips for reducing errors** in your book:

- **Use grammar software** such as ProWritingAid, Grammarly, or AutoCrit. All three have free and paid versions. (If upgrading to the paid version, search online first for discount codes.) A word of caution: there's no perfect grammar software out there. If a suggestion feels wrong, disregard it and let your editor handle it. (I love ProWritingAid, but one time, they suggested I change "the middle of the night" to "the night's middle." I got a good laugh out of it . . . and once they updated their software, they never gave me that recommendation again.)
- **Have your computer read your manuscript aloud to you.** You'll *hear* mistakes, repeated words, and awkward phrasing that you didn't *see* while revising. Depending on what type of computer you have and what software you use for drafting, there are various ways to accomplish this. (On my Mac, I set it up in the Accessibility menu within Settings.) A word of warning: listening to an entire book in a robot voice is *painfully boring*. After listening to my first book in a few mind-numbingly long sessions, I never wanted to put myself through that again. Now, I revise a single chapter, listen to it, and then revise the next chapter.
- **Read your book on a mobile device.** This is my last step before sending a manuscript to beta readers. I send the mobi version to myself and read it on my Kindle or my phone. I read next to my computer and make changes (phrasing adjustments, typo corrections) as I go. If you prefer, you can make revision notes on your device, then

go back to make changes to the document later. Reading on a new device helps your brain see things it was skipping over. I regularly make several hundred small changes to my manuscript during this step.

- **While revising based on your mobile-device read-through, turn on Track Changes.** (This applies if you're using Microsoft Word.) Track Changes uses colored text, margin notes, and more to highlight your edits. When you finish your revision round, you can review your changes before finalizing them. I use Track Changes because as I revise, I always introduce new errors. Track Changes gives me one more chance to smash those fresh worms before sending my book to betas. Need help with Track Changes? YouTube is full of tutorials.

What if you struggle with grammar, style, and typos?

First of all, that doesn't make you a bad writer. I firmly believe that storytelling and grammar are two very different skill sets. You may be an incredible storyteller who can't, for the life of you, remember where commas are supposed to go. It's okay; that's what editors are for.

Some authors pay for copy editing before starting their beta round. You may want to consider such a tactic, especially if you're confident your story is excellent and won't require major changes after the beta round. If you choose this route, a proofreader can catch last-minute errors right before you publish.

Hoping to publish traditionally? Consider a few pros and cons of paying for professional editing. We'll start with the cons.

- **Cons:** If you put your own money into editing, you may be paying for work that will be done for you at no additional charge later (*if* you pick up an agent and a

publisher). Publishing royalties are often quite low, so you may not want to incur the upfront expense of editing.
- **Pros:** If you hire a great editor, the manuscript you query will be more polished. That may help you land an agent. (Agents don't expect perfect manuscripts, but they usually won't say yes if your manuscript is really rough.) Also, an excellent editor can be a true partner, making you a better writer by teaching you more about the craft.

If you know your book likely contains a lot of worms, and you can't hire an editor to fix them, don't expect your betas to find them all. Even the most detail-oriented beta probably won't want to do a full, unpaid copy edit on your manuscript.

Need more in-depth advice on how to revise and self-edit your book? Check out "Appendix 4: Self-Editing and Revision Resources" (p. 223).

In Summary: If you work hard to polish your manuscript, your beta team can help you bring your book's quality to an even higher level.

Once your manuscript is polished, it'll be time to get it into the right format for your readers. We'll talk about that next.

PRE-BETA STEP 2: FORMAT AND CHOOSE HOW TO DISTRIBUTE YOUR MANUSCRIPT FILES

In Part 1 of the book, I suggested providing your file to early readers in **three digital formats: mobi (for Kindle), ePub, and PDF**. Check out the section titled "Formatting a Manuscript for Your Early Readers" (p. 40) to review that information. (If you want to check out formatting options in even more detail, head to "Appendix 2: File Formatting Options," p. 213.)

In Part 1, I also reviewed online services that allow you to **easily share your mobi, ePub, and PDF files with your readers**. Go back to the section titled "Providing Book Files to Readers" (p. 43) if you need a review.

In Summary: You'll need to format your manuscript and choose a website to distribute it, just as you did during the alpha phase.

Your last two pre-beta steps will help you put the right people on your team and get useful feedback from them. Keep reading to find out how.

PRE-BETA STEP 3: CREATE AN APPLICATION

We're a schnauzer family. Our dog, Ollie, is the third miniature schnauzer we've adopted over the course of seventeen years or so. (He's also the best dog we've ever had.)

The rescue agency we got Ollie through uses an online application for anyone interested in adopting. It's not a short form. It requires information on the applicant's family, their home, their other pets, their veterinarian, and more.

While I don't love filling out applications, I appreciate the organization's thoroughness. The form not only helps potential owners think through whether they're ready for a dog (*Hmm, maybe I should fix that massive hole in my fence first*), it also sends a message to the applicant: this agency takes pet ownership seriously.

Your beta reader application serves similar purposes. **It helps your potential betas think about whether they're ready to commit to beta reading, and it shows them you're serious about your book and this process.**

I first heard of the idea of using a beta reader application from Michael J. Sullivan, one of my favorite fantasy authors. I loved the idea and have used my own application for every one of my novels.

You may think, "Who am I to require a beta application? People will tell me to get off my high horse!" I feel the same way, but I've found potential betas don't push back when I ask them to fill it out. Sometimes I justify it by explaining, "This helps me keep all my info in one place."

When I was looking for betas for my first several novels, I accepted every single person who completed the application. Once I had more readers, I started getting more beta applications, and I became more selective.

Your first step will be to choose a format for your beta application. I suggest using an **online form builder**. Here are two you can consider:

- **Google Forms.** Google Forms is fairly simple to use, and it's free. It's probably the best choice for most authors.
- **Jotform**. I use Jotform because it's a website I've used in the past, and I love how flexible it is. I can even ask my betas for actual signatures (using their computer mouse or touchscreen). That being said, it's not always the simplest program to use, and their free plan has some limits.

Below is an example of a beta reader application. Like all the other templates I've shared, it's part of the resource pack you'll get of when you sign up at this link:

carolbethanderson.com/earlyreaders

Beta Reader Application for <u>*The Greatest Novel Ever*</u>

What's the "magic word" from the email or social media post where you heard about beta reading? [I'll explain what this is in the "How to Ask for Beta Readers" section. For now, simply include the question on your application.]

Name:

Email:

Do you expect to be able to read the book and provide feedback within one month of receiving it?

- Yes.
- Probably not.
- Other _____

Have you been a beta reader for me in the past?

- Yes, and I provided feedback.
- I was chosen but didn't provide feedback. (Please explain why at the end of the application.)
- No.

Have you read <u>*Title of Previous Book in Series*</u> (start to finish)?

- Yes.
- No.

How do you feel about <u>mystery novels with romantic subplots</u>?

- I love that type of book.

- I like that type of book.
- Doesn't seem like a good fit.
- I'm not sure.
- Other _____

Why do you want to be a beta reader?

What can you offer as a beta reader? (Feel free to tell me how your input might improve the book. Share any relevant skills or experience.)

If you enjoy this book, do you think you'll be available to beta read the next book in the series by next spring?

- I can probably do that.
- Maybe.
- Probably not.

If you're chosen to be a beta reader, and you complete the process in time, how would you like your name listed in the book's Acknowledgements?

If you're chosen to be a beta reader, do you agree not to share the book files with anyone and not to give pre-publication spoilers to anyone (in person or online)? (You're welcome to tell people you're a beta reader and to talk about the book without revealing important plot points.)

- Yes, I'm the hero in this story. I don't want to steal your work or give spoilers.
- No, I'm the villain in this story. I'm planning to steal your work and/or give spoilers.

How did you find out about this beta reading opportunity?

Do you have any questions or comments for me?

Please type your full name here as a signature, indicating you were truthful on this application.

Thanks so much for applying! I'll reach out to everyone who applied by February 1.

-Author Name

I ask all potential beta readers to fill out this form, even applicants who are "automatically in" (such as alpha readers or past beta readers). The application helps me stay organized. Both JotForm and Google Forms allow me to download a spreadsheet of applicants' responses.

If you aren't getting as many applications as you'd like, reach out to individuals and groups you've invited to apply, reminding them of the deadline.

At some point, you may have a strong enough beta team that you don't want to invite anyone new to join. If you're not looking for any *new* betas, I still suggest using an application, though you can shorten it significantly. An application reminds your readers of their commitment not to share your files, and it keeps you organized.

In Summary: Your beta reader application doesn't just help you choose the right betas. It also sets you up as a professional author, and it helps your betas understand their commitment.

There's one more step to take before you start your beta team. Turn the page to read about a useful tool you can use to get the feedback you need.

PRE-BETA STEP 4: CREATE A FEEDBACK FORM

I love baking sourdough bread. In fact, less than a month after I publish this book, my sourdough starter will turn five years old. If I ask my family, "What do you think of the loaf of bread I made?" I'll probably get a simple answer like, "It's good!"

But if I want real, usable feedback, I need to ask questions like, "What did you think of the crust texture?" or "How did the inside taste?"

Your beta reader feedback form is your path to real, usable feedback. If you don't ask betas specific questions, some of them may send you feedback as simple as, "This was such a good book!" Flattering? Yes. Useful? Not so much.

As with your beta reader application, you'll need to choose a form builder online. (Again, I suggest Google Forms or Jotform.)

Below is a sample beta reader feedback form.

The Greatest Novel Ever Beta Reader Feedback Form

The questions here are a starting point. You don't need to answer all of them, and you're invited to give feedback that goes beyond the questions. You can fill this out multiple times if you want to give your feedback in pieces.

It's helpful if you include quotes from the book when giving specific feedback. Just give me a few words so I can search in the document.

Your Name:

Email:

Which portion of the book are you giving feedback on? (All of it or specific chapters)

What worked for you in this book?

What didn't work for you in this book?

Are there any errors you'd like to point out?

What do you think of the book's length?

- Too long
- Too short
- Just right
- Other _____

What would you like this book to have more of? (Check all that apply) [Author, adapt the answers to fit your book/genre.]

- More romance
- More action

- More angst/emotion
- More time in characters' heads
- More worldbuilding
- Other _____

What would you like this book to have less of? (Check all that apply) [Author, adapt the answers to fit your book/genre.]

- Less romance
- Less action
- Less angst/emotion
- Less time in characters' heads
- Less worldbuilding
- Other _____

How was the pace of the book?

- Moved along quickly most or all of the time
- Hit or miss: sometimes it moved quickly, other times slowly
- Pretty slow overall
- Other _____

Which book of the series did you like best? (Please only answer if you've read all the books in this series.)

- *Book 1 Title*
- *Book 2 Title*
- I liked them the same amount
- Other _____

Fill in the blank: "I'd recommend this book for age ___ and up."

Describe a time you were emotionally affected by the plot and/or characters.

At what point of the book did you feel "hooked" on the story (if at all)?

How did you feel at the end of the book?

Please describe any parts of the book that moved slowly or where you lost interest.

The CATCH-ALL: This field is for any feedback that didn't fit somewhere else, or for general comments.

If you enjoyed this book, feel free to write a short review here that I can use in my marketing. (If I use it, I'll credit you by first name, unless you leave me different instructions.)

Are you interested in reading the next book in the series?

- Absolutely
- Probably
- Probably not
- No
- Other _____

Thank you for helping me make this book the best it can be!

-Author Name

You can **adapt this feedback form to meet your needs**. For example, for the first book in my series, I included a question asking for feedback on the book's romance, since I'd kicked it up a notch compared to my previous series.

If you have a concern about something specific, you can include a question about it. However, be careful. Leading questions can cause readers to find problems that don't exist. Instead of writing, "Did you think the violence was too gory?" you might try, "How did you react to the book's violent scenes?"

In Summary: A detailed beta feedback form will help you elicit truly useful feedback from your beta readers.

Congratulations, you've finished all the pre-beta steps! Now it's time to find some readers.

WHERE TO FIND BETA READERS

You'll search for beta readers in the same places you search for alpha readers. To refresh your memory, check out these two sections from Part 1 of the book:

- "Where to Find Alpha Readers if You Don't Have a Fan Base" (p. 19)
- "Where to Find Alpha Readers if You Have a Fan Base" (p. 22)

If you used alpha readers for your current manuscript, you've got another source of potential beta readers. I always offer to let my alpha readers beta read, and some of them take me up on it. I love hearing feedback from people who've seen the work in various phases. Recently, one of my alpha readers felt a particular scene was too long. I cut it significantly. When she read the beta version, she thought I'd gone too far. For the final draft, I found a happy medium between the rambling alpha version of the scene and its stripped-down beta counterpart.

In Part 1, I suggested you select who to invite to your alpha team, rather than putting out public calls for readers. That's because you should trust someone before giving them your rough draft.

However, if your beta drafts are high quality, you can feel more confident about sharing them. The beta phase is a great time to discover new early readers, people you might not have thought to individually invite.

My advice is this: **Cast a wide net,** *then* **choose which beta readers are a good fit.**

You can still personally ask some individuals whose feedback you want. In addition, I suggest putting out public calls for beta readers in these places:

- **Your newsletter** (If you don't have one, check out the article, "0 to 1,000+ mailing list subscribers" on StoryOrigin's blog.)
- **Your social media** (author-related and, if you wish, personal accounts).
- **Other book-related communities** you're part of, if such self-promo is encouraged. Maybe you're in a book club or a Facebook group for readers in your genre. Be sure to check with group leaders before asking for betas.
- If your book needs **fact checking** (historical, vocational, scientific, etc.), you may want to include at least one specialist on your beta team. Let's say your main character is a meteorologist. Consider asking friends if they know someone in that field who might join your team. If you can't find a friend of a friend who fits the bill, search online and start sending emails.

Some authors fear that if they bring in too many beta readers, they'll lose paying customers. However, in my experience, betas often turn into enthusiastic fans. A good number of them buy my books once I've published, and some of them spread the word on social media. I don't think I lose that many sales by having a big beta team. If I do, it's worth it, because betas make my books better, likely resulting in *more* readers in the end.

One more note about finding beta readers: **if you write for teens or kids**, it may help to reach out to parents or teachers who can connect you with young betas. (Note, however, that a large number of readers of "teen/YA" fiction are actually adults. And some adults will have great feedback on books written for younger kids too. Don't hesitate to bring adults onto your beta team if you write for younger audiences.)

In Summary: I suggest casting a wide net for beta reader applicants. You can reach out to potential readers through your newsletter, social media, other book-related communities, etc.

Now that you have a plan for *where* to find betas, we'll cover *how* to encourage them to apply.

HOW TO ASK FOR BETA READERS

Potential beta readers need to know what they're getting into. Otherwise, they may volunteer, then never follow through.

You'll want to provide potential betas with a **detailed description of how beta reading works**. There are several ways to post this description online:

- **Blog post or website page**
- **Public Facebook post**
- **Email newsletter** (Many newsletter services provide a permalink that leads people to a website with your newsletter's content. You can email your subscribers, then share the link to the email on social media.)
- **Google Docs**

I use a combination of methods: an email for my newsletter and, for everyone else, a link to a page on my website.

Below is a sample request for beta reader applicants.

Subject line [if using email]: <u>Name</u>, would you like to apply as a beta reader for my next novel?

By <u>February 1</u>, I'll be ready for beta readers for my next <u>mystery</u> novel.

At the bottom of this <u>email or post</u>, there's a link to apply to be a beta reader. **But before you fill out that form, please read ALL of the following explanation.**

Explanation: What is a beta reader?

Beta readers **read a book early**, before it's in its completed form. (There will be errors and rough spots in the book.)

Beta readers **give detailed feedback** by a specific deadline. (You'll have a full month after I send you the ebook. I'll give you a feedback form to fill out, and you're also welcome to provide feedback in another format.)

Beta readers **follow instructions.** (For instance, I asked you to read this email before applying, so you've already got this part down! The beta reader application will ask you for a "magic word." That word is "<u>WORMS</u>.")

A little bit about this book:

Title: <u>*The Greatest Novel Ever*</u>. [You can also post the cover here if you'd like.]

Book 1: <u>This is the second book in my "Mysteries and Marvels" series.</u>

Length: Full-length novel, around <u>80,000</u> words

Genre: <u>Mystery with some romance on the side</u>

Content: I'd rate it PG-13. It contains some non-gory violence, mild language, and non-explicit romantic scenes. There are also some descriptions of physical abuse. [List any content here that may be traumatic or troubling to readers.]

Selection Process: I limit the size of my beta reading team, and I'll choose those who seem most likely to be good fits for this particular book. However, everyone is welcome to join My Reader Group on Facebook. Group members get free early copies of my ebooks to review. Click here {link} to join.

Beta reading **is a big deal.** I depend on my beta readers to bring me crucial feedback, because **I want to write and sell good books.**

Beta reading is a free gig and comes with a huge amount of my appreciation. Complete your beta-reading mission, and I'll list your name in my book's Acknowledgements.

If this doesn't sound like a good fit, **that's 100% okay.** Honestly, beta reading probably isn't a good fit for a lot of people.

But if you've made it this far and are thinking, "This is right up my alley," click here {link} to fill out the application to become a beta reader. Please fill it out by January 30, and make sure you've read all of the above explanation first.

Thanks for being interested in my books!

-Your Name

Your post or email may look different from this. That's fine. Whatever verbiage you use, **I urge you not to skip this step.** I've heard story after story from authors whose beta readers don't follow through. There are lots of reasons for this, but I'm convinced **communication is key**. How can we expect someone to follow through with a task if they don't understand what they're signing up for?

If you're **only inviting past betas to return**, you can shorten this description significantly. They already know how you work, but you'll want to tell them a little about the book, what the timeline is, etc.

In Summary: When you ask people to apply as beta readers, give them lots of details about the book and the beta reading process.

When your beta application deadline rolls around, it'll be time to form your team. We'll cover that in the next section.

CHOOSING YOUR BETA READERS

How big should your beta team be? Well, some authors choose only one beta reader, and I came across one author who had over a hundred! **I suggest shooting for a minimum of five and a maximum of twenty-five beta readers.**

I know, I know . . . that's a huge range. Let me explain my thinking.

When you develop your first beta reader team and follow the guidelines in this book, you can reasonably expect half of them to follow through. If you choose five beta readers, you can expect feedback from two or three.

What about that upper limit of twenty-five? Well, when it comes to beta teams, I'm a little bit . . . extra. Okay, maybe a lot extra. As I mentioned in the Introduction, I had twenty-eight betas for one of my recent books. Yep, you read that right. I enjoy working with a large team, but it's not a good strategy for everyone. Here are some things to consider if you're thinking about forming a big beta team.

Pros of a having a large beta team:

- You're more likely to end up with at least **a few *priceless* betas** . . . the types that give particularly helpful, practical feedback.
- Feedback is data. **With plenty of data, you can better determine whether to change something.** (If one of your two beta readers said the book was slow, it might be a fluke. If ten of your twenty beta readers said it was slow . . . it probably was.)
- **The more beta readers you have, the more worms they'll catch.** Some errors are obvious. Twelve betas may point out that you called your character by the wrong name for two pages straight. However, minor continuity errors and obscure grammar errors are harder to find, and a large beta team is more likely to include someone who picks up on them.
- **Beta readers often end up being the biggest fans of your work.** They feel invested, and hopefully they'll spread the word to their friends.

Cons of having a large beta team:

- **It's overwhelming.** My betas provide me with thousands of words of feedback. Organizing all of it is stressful. For me, it's worth it, because it makes my book better. You may have a different experience.
- **It could be confusing.** You may end up with "too many cooks in the kitchen." More betas lead to more contradictory feedback, and it can be hard to decide what changes to make with so many diverse opinions.

In suggesting you choose up to twenty-five betas, I'm falling into that old parenting habit: "Do as I say, not as I do." Twenty-eight betas is excessive. Somehow, I made it work for me, but it was honestly overwhelming. I don't know if I'll have a team that large again.

If it's your first book, you likely won't get twenty-five volunteers. However, if at some point you build a team that big, and at least twelve to fifteen of them give you feedback, you'll quickly learn how well you handle a large beta team. From there, you can decide if you want to grow it further or cull it down for your next book.

How do you decide to shoot for a team of five, twenty-five, or somewhere in between? A whole lot of this comes down to personality. Go with what feels right, and adjust as needed with your subsequent books. (Remember that if you do want a large team, it may take several books to build up to it.)

If you're lucky enough to get more applications than you need, you'll have to make some tough choices. Here are several **factors to consider when choosing your team:**

- **Diversity of strengths.** I ask applicants what they can offer as betas, because I want both big-picture people (who will tell me if pacing sucks and characters are annoying) and detail people (who will tell me if my spelling sucks and my comma usage is annoying).
- **Target audience.** Most of your beta team members should be the types of people you expect to read your book. Consider age group, who enjoys the genre, etc.
- **How well they follow directions.** In my beta reader description post, I list a "magic word," which I then ask for on the application. If someone doesn't read the instructions fully and find that magic word, they also may not read my beta emails . . . or my book.
- **Past membership on your alpha or beta teams.** If

applicants have already proven their reliability and helpfulness, I suggest you accept them onto your team again.
- **Positivity.** Don't stack your team with people who give only positive feedback. However, if you're the sensitive sort (as I am), it's okay to have one or two team members who are rabid fans of your work and mostly tell you how amazing you are! Those gushing words may help temper the emotional effect of useful, yet difficult critiques from other team members.

You may wish to invite some fellow authors to apply for your beta team. You can read more about that strategy by revisiting the section from Part 1 titled, "Pros and Cons of Asking Fellow Authors to be Early Readers" (p. 25).

In Summary: Once you know how many beta readers you want (I suggest five to twenty-five), select those who are likely to give you the best, most comprehensive feedback.

In the next two sections, we'll talk about communicating with all your applicants, whether they make the team or not.

COMMUNICATING WITH BETA APPLICANTS WHO DON'T MAKE THE TEAM

Saying no to an eager potential beta reader isn't easy. However, you may find it necessary, in order to keep your team size manageable.

If you're lucky enough to get more applicants than you need (or if some applicants simply don't fit your criteria), **make sure to communicate with those you didn't choose.** They're eager to read your words! You want them as fans, even if they aren't on your beta team.

Here's the best way to respond to those who don't make the team:

Invite them to be ARC readers.

If someone wants early access to my books as a beta reader, but I don't choose them for that role, I want to transfer that enthusiasm to my ARC team. (A large ARC team is *way* easier to manage than a large beta team.)

Reach out to every beta applicant you don't choose. Here's a sample email:

Subject line: Update on beta reading

Thank you for applying to be a beta reader for *The Greatest Novel Ever*. I had more applicants than spots available, and unfortunately, I didn't add you to my team this time around. I think you'd have fantastic input, but I need to limit the number of readers to keep my process manageable.

Instead of being on my beta team, I invite you to join my ARC team. That means you'll get a digital ARC (Advance Review Copy) before the book publishes. I'll ask you to review the book, and I'll even have a contest to see who can catch the most grammatical errors and typos. ARC readers get to read the book early, for free. I'm excited to invite you onto that team!

I've set up an email list to notify you when ARCs are ready. **To sign up early for my review team, just click here: {link}.**

And if you haven't yet joined my reader community on Facebook, My Amazing Reader Group, check it out here: {link}.

Thanks again for your enthusiastic support of my novels! I appreciate you wanting to help me make them better.

-Your Name

Note that I ask them to click a link if they want to be an ARC reader. To generate that link, I use my email service to set up a list for those who want to be ARC readers. I then set up a landing page on my website where they can sign up for that list.

If you prefer not to take this step, you can instead tell them you'll reach out again when ARC copies are ready. Then be sure to follow through.

Here's a tip to protect your readers' privacy: communicate using individual emails, BCC (blind carbon copy), or the email service you use for your author newsletter.

In Summary: When you don't accept an applicant onto your beta team, offer them a place on your ARC team.

Saying no can be tough. Let's move on to a task that's a lot more fun: connecting with those who made the team.

WELCOMING YOUR NEW BETA READERS

Whether you're saying yes to twenty-five percent of your beta applicants or to all of them, *you chose them*. It's time to congratulate them for making the team.

Your welcome email to your beta readers is one of your most crucial pieces of communication through this whole process.

- It gives your beta readers one place to return to with **all the information they need**.
- It sets **specific expectations** so that betas are more likely to follow through.
- The **professionalism** of this communication sets the standard for the rest of your beta process.

Be sure to communicate using individual emails, BCC (blind carbon copy), or the email service you use for your author newsletter. Your brand-new betas might not be thrilled if you share their email addresses with the whole team.

Below is a welcome-email example.

Subject line: <u>Name</u>, congrats, you're in as a beta reader!

Congratulations! I've chosen you as a beta reader for <u>The Greatest Novel Ever</u>. Thank you for applying.

Don't delete this; it's the big email with all the important info in it.

Please get feedback to me by the end of the night on <u>March 1</u>. That gives you <u>one month</u>. I'll keep in touch with you once a week between now and then.

IMPORTANT LINKS:

- Ebook/PDF Download {link}
- Feedback form {link}

WHICH VERSION SHOULD YOU CHOOSE, AND HOW WILL YOU KEEP TRACK OF FEEDBACK AS YOU READ?

Ebook:

- If you want a **digital reading experience on a handheld device**, download the ebook and read it on your e-reader, tablet, or phone.
- In the ebook, you can **highlight and type notes**. Later you can pull up your notes and highlights and send them to me.
- If you want to **take notes on a Kindle** and send the notes to me, **you'll need to follow special book-download instructions**. Please click this link before downloading, so you don't end up with a Kindle full of notes you can't export. carolbethanderson.com/how-to-take-and-export-kindle-notes/

PDF:

- If you want to **read on your computer or print the book**, this is a good option.

Word/Google Docs:

- If you prefer to read in Microsoft Word or Google Docs so you can leave comments in the document itself, just email me.

Keep the book confidential, no matter what form you read it in.

HOW/WHEN TO GIVE FEEDBACK:

You can give feedback **in chunks** as you read **or all at once** at the end.

Feel free to email me with feedback any time.

I've also made a feedback form with suggested questions.

- Click here for the feedback form {link}, which you can fill out as many times as you'd like (for parts of the book or the whole book).
- The form covers specific areas where I'm looking for guidance, so I'd love for you to fill it out, even if you're providing feedback in another format too.
- **Please review the form before you start the book. It will help guide your critical mind as you read.**

Remember the deadline, [insert day of week and date].

FEEDBACK GUIDELINES:

- I welcome both **positive feedback** and **constructive criticism**.
- Be specific. Please **provide several words from the book** when giving feedback on a specific passage. That way, I can search my manuscript for those words. (Please don't give me the page number or ebook location number.)
- **Content or grammar?** As I've worked with beta readers, I've found that some naturally give "bigger" feedback on content, and others have eagle eyes for errors in grammar, punctuation, etc. I appreciate both types of feedback.

One more thing—**if you enjoy this book, feel free to "talk it up" on social media.** It's on pre-order [insert links if applicable], and you can also add it to your Goodreads [insert link if applicable].

Let me know if you have any questions.

-Your Name

P.S. You ROCK! Thank you for spending your time to make this book better.

P.P.S. A reminder for those who plan to take notes on the Kindle version: please follow these instructions to be sure you don't lose your notes:

carolbethanderson.com/how-to-take-and-export-kindle-notes/

When you write your own email, you're welcome to send readers to my website for those Kindle note instructions, or you can copy and paste the instructions onto your own website.

You may be reading that email and thinking, *Wow, that's long!* And you're right. I send lots of instructions upfront so beta readers feel equipped to do their jobs well; and I **use formatting (bold, italics, bullet points) to keep the information readable**.

In the "Pre-Beta Step 1" section, we discussed polishing up your manuscript before sending it to betas. If you know your beta manuscript still needs a lot of editing, then in your welcome email, you can delete the part encouraging betas to send grammar corrections. Instead, say something like, "This is an early version of the manuscript. Please ignore typos and grammar errors. An editor will handle those later."

Don't send this email unless your book files are ready. If they aren't ready when your application deadline arrives, you can send a quick note to your team to congratulate them and tell them when they'll be hearing from you again. Then when the files are ready, you can send the long, information-packed email.

In Summary: Your beta-welcome email should be packed with information so that your betas have everything they need to feel successful as early readers.

Your welcome email is a major part of your strategy for encouraging beta readers to complete their task. In the next section, we'll discuss another way to optimize follow-through.

THE KEY TO BETA READER FOLLOW-THROUGH

I've heard it over and over on Twitter and Facebook: "My beta readers don't follow through! I sent them my manuscript, and they fell off the face of the Earth!"

You can't expect perfect follow-through from your betas. However, if you've got a good book and a good beta process, at least half will likely follow through. (I consider them to have followed through even if they only provide feedback on part of the book. Life happens.)

As you move on to additional books, and some of your betas stay on your team, your follow-through percentage should improve.

The key to improving follow-through is these three words:

Communicate. Communicate. Communicate.

If you sent out detailed information to potential applicants and sent out an in-depth email to accepted applicants, you're off to a great start.

During the beta reading phase, I suggest you **email your beta readers once a week**. (I email all of mine, even those who've already given feedback. They're still part of the team.)

Keep these emails short. **Send them as replies to your welcome email**, so your betas once again have all the information they need (such as links to the files and the feedback form) at their fingertips.

My weekly email might go something like this:

Subject line: Quick reminder to beta readers

Hi, beta readers! This is your weekly reminder email. **You've still got 2 weeks until your deadline of March 1, but you're welcome to send feedback early if you're ready.**

Thank you to those of you who've already shared your thoughts with me!

Below is your welcome email. Consult it for all the details, and let me know if you have any questions.

I'd love for you to fill out the feedback form {link}, even if you're giving me feedback in another format too.

Thanks for helping make this book the best it can be.

-Your Name

In my final weekly email before the due date, I add something like this:

I know life gets busy, and unexpected things happen. If you don't think you'll be able to complete your beta reading, please let me know. I promise, I'll understand! If you were able to read part of the book, I'd love your feedback on that portion. Before too long, I'll open up my ARC (Advance Review Copy) team for readers who'd like an early digital copy to review. If you'd rather be on my ARC team instead of my beta team, just ask.

The day before your deadline, send one more reminder. Here's an example:

Subject line: TOMORROW is the deadline for beta feedback

Hello to the best betas on Earth! **Tomorrow is your deadline for providing beta feedback.**

Thank you so much to those who've already provided feedback. In case you haven't filled it out yet, here's a link to the feedback form {link}.

-Your Name

You can end the email with the same "I know life gets busy" paragraph from above.

The day after your deadline, I suggest reaching out individually to anyone you haven't heard from. Say something like this:

Subject line: <u>Name</u>, I'd love an update from you

Hi, <u>Name</u>! It looks like I haven't gotten beta reading feedback from you, and I wanted to check in. Is everything okay? I'd love to hear an update from you.

One more time, insert the "I know life gets busy" paragraph.

Occasionally, betas will ghost you. They may be embarrassed they didn't fulfill their commitment. That's okay. But if you touch base frequently, you'll probably get explanations from most of those who didn't send feedback.

A lot of authors are nervous to reach out to beta readers. We don't want to annoy them . . . and we're nervous about getting their critiques.

However, think of it from a beta reader's point of view. If you send them a manuscript and they never hear from you again, they may come across it one day and think, "Oh yeah, I forgot about this. I guess it's too late. I never heard from the author, so they probably found other readers." They might feel a little uncomfortable. You'll feel more than a little disappointed. No one wins. Do your readers and yourself the favor of sending gentle reminders.

To avoid nagging, **keep your communications positive and (except for the welcome email) short.** Your beta readers will appreciate you treating them like the important team members they are.

In Summary: The key to improving beta feedback is communication. I suggest short, weekly emails during the beta

process, along with last-minute reminders for all, and requests for updates from those who don't meet the deadline.

If you communicate with your team well, a good percentage of them will likely follow through. In the next section, we'll discuss how to respond to their critiques.

RESPONDING TO BETA FEEDBACK

I always respond to beta reader feedback.

I used to think it was enough to send a simple (and exuberant) thank-you email. However, I do quite a bit of beta reading, and when I only get a "thank you" from the author, I always wonder if they're actually utilizing any of the feedback I took so much time to provide.

These days, I try to give more detailed feedback to every beta reader. I thank them, and I try to hit on *at least* one or two specific critiques I found helpful. If I need clarification on something they said, I ask for it. Occasionally, I ask a beta what they think of my solution to the problem they pointed out.

If I'm not planning to review a beta's feedback in detail until later, I still send them a note thanking them and confirming I received it. Later, when I dig into their notes, I email them with more specific gratitude.

When you send every beta your personalized thanks and let them know that their notes are making your book better, you're cultivating relationships with them that may extend across numerous books.

In Summary: Send personalized, detailed responses to your beta readers so they know their feedback is making a difference.

Next, we'll discuss what to do with the feedback your betas provide.

ORGANIZING AND EVALUATING BETA FEEDBACK AND REVISING YOUR MANUSCRIPT

I use the same organization system for beta feedback that I use for alpha feedback. Head to the "How to Organize Feedback" section (p. 57) to review my system.

However, beta feedback tends to be more voluminous than alpha feedback, at least for me. That's because my team is larger, and I invite them to give me detailed critiques, including grammatical corrections, etc.

To save time, as I review beta feedback, I immediately fix the typos and grammar/style errors my readers pointed out, instead of copying and pasting them into a Word document. It's faster to fix those tiny errors and forget them. I use my Word document to organize feedback that requires more rewriting. Then, once I've compiled it all, I jump back into my manuscript and revise it.

Not all feedback is created equal. As with alpha feedback, you'll evaluate each piece of beta feedback and decide whether to heed it. For guidance on how to do this, head back to the "Deciding Which Feedback to Utilize When Revising" section (p. 55).

Because this book focuses on early reader systems, I won't go into further detail on how to revise your manuscript. However, you'll find useful suggestions in "Appendix 3: A Sample Early Reading, Revision, and Editing Process" (p. 221) and "Appendix 4: Self-Editing and Revision Resources" (p. 223).

I have one practical, post-beta revision tip: **turn on Microsoft Word's Track Changes feature before you revise** (just as I suggested you do in your last round of post-alpha revisions). It'll help you avoid introducing too many new errors. Check out YouTube's tutorials if you're not sure how to use this tool.

In Summary: Once your beta feedback comes in, you'll need to organize it and decide which feedback to utilize. Then it'll be time to revise your manuscript.

Revisions are tough. Knowing when to stop revising can be even tougher. That's the topic of our next section.

HOW TO KNOW YOUR POST-BETA REVISIONS ARE DONE

If I'm making a holiday feast, I create a to-do list to keep me on track. Ideally, I move through that to-do list sequentially, and I finish everything on time.

Ideally.

More realistically, there's a good chance I'll forget stuff (*Oh yeah, I need to set the table*), or unexpected complications will muck things up (*Is the gravy supposed to be lumpy?*).

Similarly, I have a book-writing process, but it doesn't always go as planned. Ideally, when I finish post-beta revisions, the book is ready for ARC readers.

However, sometimes, I need multiple beta rounds. One time I got fancy and called the extra round a "gamma round." (Yes, I did have to Google "3rd letter of the Greek alphabet" before I named it that.)

How do you know if you need another round of beta reading (AKA gamma reading)?

I like to do a new round if I'm making *major* changes, like significant plot adjustments. I try to get those big changes out of the way during post-alpha revisions. Twice, however, I've gotten difficult (and helpful) critiques from betas, pointing out big worms that led to major rewrites.

As soon as you realize you're going to need another round of beta reading, let your beta team know. Some of them may have procrastinated, and they'll be happy to delay their beta reading until you have a new manuscript for them. Others may want to read in both rounds. You may need to search for new readers if you don't have enough who want to continue with the second round.

Whether I do one or two rounds of beta reading, **I know my post-beta revisions are done when the book is compelling and polished, and when I've corrected as many errors as I can.** There's no such thing as a perfect book, so I try to write books that are **as good as they can reasonably be, considering my current level of skill.**

I say "as good as they can reasonably be," because it's possible to get caught in a never-ending revision cycle. Reading your manuscript fifty times is probably not reasonable! Work hard on your revisions so you can end up with an excellent, professional product... and then move on.

In Summary: If you realize your book needs major changes, you may want to have more than one round of beta reading. The goal of your post-beta revisions is excellence, not perfection.

Let's wrap up the beta reading section with ideas of how to make these strategies work for you.

THE BETA READER PHASE: MAKE IT YOUR OWN

However you organize your beta phase, I suggest you don't compromise on these priorities:

- **Set clear expectations.**
- **Communicate well.**

Beyond that, have fun creating your own strategies. Here are some ideas to get you started:

- I've heard from authors who **provide sample chapters** to potential beta readers. That way, people who don't like the story or writing style can weed themselves out.
- Some authors use **Google Docs** for their beta phase, asking readers to leave comments in the document. (To be honest, I find Google Docs frustrating to use as a beta reader. But your betas may disagree. You may want to check with them before going this route.)
- An author friend (Mackenzie Littledale) chose a small, select group of beta readers and mailed them **physical**

copies of her manuscript, printed at a print shop. She asked the readers to mail them back. It added an extra level of security to her process.
- Some authors use **paid beta readers**. If you have the budget for it, it's a valid option. Do your homework first, to be sure the betas you're hiring have proven themselves reliable and helpful to past clients.
- If you prefer not to organize every aspect of your beta process yourself, consider two website/apps, betabooks.co and betareader.io, that provide dedicated platforms for facilitating your beta reading process. They tie your readers to particular reading apps, which some of them may not like. But both have nice features and add security to the beta reading process.

In Summary: There are plenty of ways to modify your beta phase. Just make sure you never compromise on setting clear expectations and communicating well.

Congratulations! You now have the knowledge you need to build teams of reliable, helpful alpha and beta readers.

In Part 3 of the book, we'll discuss strategies for building your third team of early readers: your ARC team.

PART 3
ARC READERS

ARC READERS OVERVIEW

Recently, I came across a one-star review of one of my novels. The reviewer called a major character "whiny" and insisted that most of the four- and five-star reviews must've come from friends and family. (Thankfully, that assumption was false.)

With the possibility of such gut-wrenching critiques, why would we actually *ask* for reviews? Because if you've written a good book, *most* reviewers will praise it. The book with the "whiny" character also has dozens of four-star and five-star reviews.

Plus, having a couple of one-star and two-star reviews can give your book more credibility. (They prove that your book isn't only being read by people who adore you in real life.)

You don't have to sit around and wait for reviews from customers who purchase your book. **About a month to six weeks before you publish, you can give away ARCs (Advance Review Copies)** to individuals who agree to read and review.

Why have ARC readers?

- Reviews can give a book credibility, and building an ARC team can give you a **head start on building up those review numbers**.
- ARC readers can help **generate interest** for a book (if they post about it on social media, for instance).
- ARC readers can provide you with **pre-launch reviews to quote in your marketing**.
- Sometimes **ARC readers point out errors** you can fix before a book is published.

A couple of notes about this section of the book, before we move on to all the practical advice:

- **I mostly give out digital (ebook) ARCs**, rather than paperback or hardcover ARCs. Always assume I'm talking about digital ARCs unless I say otherwise.
- Most of the advice in this section is for **self-published authors. (An author published by a small, indie publisher** may also find parts of it useful, if the publisher gives their authors latitude in how the ARC phase is run.)
- This book will focus on getting reviews on **retail sites** (such as Amazon), rather than on other sites (like book blogs). In my opinion, it's best for self-published authors to focus most of their efforts during the ARC phase on getting reviews in the places where readers shop for books. I'll also give some tips for connecting with reviewers on Instagram, since so many readers spend time there.

In Summary: ARC readers provide authors with early reviews and social media buzz. They may even report typos before

publication. This section of the book is written primarily for self- and indie-published authors.

You have some important steps to take before inviting people to review your book. We'll cover those in the next several sections.

PRE-ARC STEP 1: MAKE YOUR BOOK SHINE

One of your pre-beta steps was to polish up your manuscript. Before you send your book to ARC readers, you'll need to polish it even more, until it truly shines. **Your ARC version should be *very* close to your final version.**

ARC readers usually expect some typos. But if you've got typos on every page, some readers will struggle to look past that. If you suspect you have a lot of errors, you may need to use a professional proofreader *before* releasing your ARC.

For practical suggestions on producing a quality book, check out "Appendix 3: A Sample Early Reading, Revision, and Editing Process (p. 221).

The *outside* of your book needs to shine at this phase too. You need a great, genre-appropriate cover. It can help you connect to the right reviewers, those who love your genre. If you're not sure if your cover is doing the trick, get feedback on it. I suggest two Facebook cover-critique groups: Indie Cover Project and The Cover Clinic.

In Summary: The ARC version of your book should be highly polished with very few errors. An excellent cover can attract reviewers too.

Before reaching out to ARC readers, you need to decide where you want them to review. We'll cover that next.

PRE-ARC STEP 2: REVIEW SITES

Before you ever reach out to potential ARC readers, take time to consider **where you want them to review**. Below are various websites that accept reviews. We'll discuss what steps to take on these sites before your ARC phase starts.

Here's a tricky part of the ARC process: different sites allow reviews at different phases of the process. For instance, Goodreads lets readers review unpublished books, but Amazon only allows reviews of published books. Each heading below includes information on when the site allows reviews.

AMAZON (ALLOWS REVIEWS OF PUBLISHED BOOKS ONLY)

Amazon sells far more books than any other retailer. Reviews there are very important.

Authors who are self-publishing, you've got a decision to make: what's your Amazon release strategy? Here are a few release strategies to consider:

- **Option 1: Set up a pre-order.** You can set up **ebook pre-orders** directly through KDP or through your chosen distributor (such as Draft2Digital). KDP Print doesn't allow **paperback pre-orders**, but IngramSpark and various other paperback distributors do. (For my Amazon paperback listings, I use both IngramSpark and KDP. Check out the blog post titled "Using Both KDP & IngramSpark for Paperback Printing" at carolbethanderson.com.)
- **Option 2: Publish your book on the day of release (no pre-order).** If you choose this route, you won't get an Amazon link until launch day.
- **Option 3: Set a public launch date, but do a "soft launch" for reviewers.** In a soft launch, you publish the paperback and/or ebook a few days before your public release date. During this "soft launch," share your Amazon link with reviewers only. This is a good way to get some Amazon reviews before you publicly release your book.

There are pros and cons to each of these options. Detailed release strategies are beyond the scope of this book, but there are countless articles and books available on the topic. Regardless of which option you choose, **as soon as you have an Amazon link, take note of it.**

BOOKBUB (ALLOWS REVIEWS OF PRE-ORDER AND PUBLISHED BOOKS)

BookBub is a site that allows authors to promote their books (and allows readers to review them). Check out their site to see all their options. As an author, you can become a BookBub Partner and claim your book on their site.

- **Sign up as a BookBub Partner for free** by visiting partners.bookbub.com/
- Once your book is on pre-order or published, claim it on BookBub under "My Books." **Take note of the link.** If you're not doing a pre-order, make a note to complete this step on release day.
- Unlike Amazon, BookBub **allows ARC readers to review books that are on pre-order.**

GOODREADS (ALLOWS REVIEWS OF *ANY* BOOK *ANY* TIME—EVEN IF IT'S NOT PUBLISHED OR ON PRE-ORDER)

Goodreads is a social media site for readers. You'll probably get more reviews there than on Amazon, as they accept reviews from anyone. Below are instructions on how to list your book on Goodreads and become a Goodreads Author. (You can do this whether or not your book is on pre-order.)

- **Set up a Goodreads account** if you don't already have one.
- **Search for your book.** (If it's on pre-order on Amazon, it may already be on Goodreads. Or one of your alpha or beta readers may have added it manually.) If it's there, you can edit it (add a description, cover, etc.).
- If your book isn't yet on Goodreads, you can "**add a new record**" (add the book to their database). **You can add your book even if you're not doing a pre-order.**
- **Take note of your Goodreads book link.**
- If your book is on pre-order, **apply to become a Goodreads Author.** (If you're not doing a pre-order, take this step and the next one once your book is released.)
- **If your book doesn't show up under your author

profile, post in the Goodreads Librarian Group to ask that it be added.
- Even if your book isn't on pre-order, **your ARC readers can review there as soon as they're done reading**.

OTHER RETAILERS

Let's briefly talk about three other major ebook retailers.

- **Barnes & Noble** (mostly U.S. customers, **allows reviews on pre-orders and published books**)
- **Kobo** (international, **allows reviews on published books only**)
- **Apple Books** (international, **allows reviews on pre-orders and published books**)

If you're distributing your book to these or any other ebook sellers, **take note of each retailer's link to your book** once you've published or put the book on pre-order.

In Summary: Before starting your ARC phase, choose which sites you'll ask your readers to review on. Set up your pre-order on Amazon (if you choose to have one); and set up your profiles on Goodreads and BookBub.

I've told you throughout this section to make note of your book links on various sites. Next, we'll discuss how to keep those links organized.

PRE-ARC STEP 3: ORGANIZE YOUR LINKS

As an author, you have many links to keep track of—most importantly, links to your books on various sites. **I suggest using a note-taking app that syncs across your computer and mobile devices to organize all these links.** That way, any time you need a link, you can easily find it and copy it.

Consider saving your links on one of these free note-taking apps:

- **Google Keep**
- **Microsoft OneNote**
- **Apple Notes** (access through Apple device apps or the iCloud website)

You can save other publishing- and marketing-related links on these apps too, such as links to your social media profiles. For more detailed suggestions about links you may want to save, check out my blog post titled "Organize Your Marketing Links" at carolbethanderson.com.

In Summary: Use a free note-taking app so your book links are always close at hand.

Once your book is set up on various sites, and you've organized your links, it's time to convert your manuscript into a reader-friendly format. Keep reading for tips.

PRE-ARC STEP 4: FORMATTING YOUR ARC

In the alpha and beta sections of this book, I suggested making mobile-friendly formats (epub, mobi, and PDF) available to your early readers. However, some of you will choose other formats during those phases (such as Google Docs).

Once you reach the ARC phase, reader-friendly/mobile-friendly formatting is a must. Your ARC readers aren't there to dig deep into a manuscript like early readers are. Reviewers want to enjoy the reading process, and that means they need well-formatted digital copies, just like the ebooks they purchase.

If you're self-publishing, you'll need to format your own ARCs. Head back to "Formatting a Manuscript for Your Early Readers" (p. 40) to review your formatting options.

I suggest adding a special instruction page to the beginning *and* end of your ARC manuscript. It can look something like this:

EARLY READERS CATCH THE WORMS

ARC READER FAQs

Thank you for reading and reviewing!

• **What's an ARC?** An Advance Review Copy. It's not a final copy, and there may be a few lingering typos.

• **What are the review links?** Amazon, Goodreads, BookBub. {Insert links, plus any other sites where you want them to review.} [If your book is not available for pre-order, you won't have Amazon or BookBub links yet. Tell your readers you'll provide those once the book launches.]

• **What if I find a typo?** Rather than mentioning it in a review, please mark it and let me know. You can email me at author-name@mysite.com. Please give me the chapter number and several words so I can find the typo. Whoever finds the most valid errors by April 6 will get a signed paperback copy of my book (or an unsigned copy if you live outside the US). If there's a tie, I'll draw one winner. And *everyone* who submits typos will get a signed bookmark.

• **When should I review?** On Amazon {link}, please review as soon as the book is published (April 13). If you finish early, **please review before publication** on other sites.

• **Who should review on Amazon?** Anyone who can . . . *unless* you're my close friend or close family member or a fellow author I have a personal relationship with. Amazon prohibits such reviews.

• **How many stars should I give the book?** As many as you honestly feel it deserves!

• **Verified reviews on Amazon:** Feel like purchasing the book on Amazon {link} so your review will be Verified? I never expect

ARC reviewers to do so, but if you'd like to . . . wow, thanks!

•**Do I need a disclaimer in my review?** Yes, unless you purchase the book. *Please don't say you were given the book "in exchange for" a review.* Suggested language: "I received a complimentary copy of this book and am leaving an honest review."

•**What if I don't want to finish the book?** That's okay. No book is a perfect fit for every reader.

•**What else can I do to support you?** How kind of you to ask. If you liked this book, please post about it on social media. You can also sign up for my newsletter {link}. [Note: also highlight any freebie they'll get when they sign up for your newsletter]. Lastly, I'd love for you to join my Facebook reader group, My Reader Group, at {link}.

Thanks again!

-Your Name

See the mention of a typo contest? We'll discuss that in more detail soon.

By putting this reminder at the beginning and end of the book, you're giving ARC readers all the important information in one place . . . and you're reminding them they aren't *just* reading for fun; they need to leave a review too.

In Summary: ARC readers want to read books in mobile-friendly formats. You can include special review instructions at the beginning and end of your ARCs.

Once you have a formatted book, complete with instructions for your readers, you'll need a way to distribute it. We'll discuss your options in the next section.

PRE-ARC STEP 5: CHOOSE A DISTRIBUTION SERVICE

Just as with alpha and beta manuscripts, you'll need a great way to distribute your digital ARCs. Here are four options:

Option 1: BookFunnel or ProlificWorks

- **Remember BookFunnel and ProlificWorks**, two of the sites that allow you to distribute alpha and beta manuscripts to readers? (Head back to "Providing Book Files to Readers," p. 43, for a refresher.) You can use either of these sites to provide downloads of your ARCs.
- **Pros:** Use your existing membership. No need to learn to navigate a new service.
- **Cons:** These sites won't find reviewers for you. You'll also be responsible for 100% of your reminder communications to ARC readers.

Option 2: StoryOrigin

- **StoryOrigin**, another site I recommended earlier, has a

more full-service ARC program than BookFunnel or Prolific Works.
- **Pros:** With StoryOrigin's Review Copy feature, you can check out a reviewer's past reliability before approving them. StoryOrigin sends a review reminder to your ARC readers. They also provide you with email addresses of those who review your book with at least three stars, so you can invite them to review future books. Lastly, StoryOrigin keeps track of who's reviewed and gives you that information.
- **Cons:** StoryOrigin won't find reviewers for you. They also don't give you email addresses when reviewers sign up, so you can't send out your own reminders. (If you want to use StoryOrigin and send your own reminders, use their Reader Magnets service instead. You'll lose the other features of the Review Copy service.)

Option 3: Booksprout

- **Booksprout** is a full-featured ARC service for authors and publishers. They have free and paid plans.
- **Pros:** Pay monthly (if using a paid plan), and cancel when you're not using it. Booksprout will send reminders to your ARC readers plus provide you with email addresses so you can send your own reminders. On both free and paid plans, Booksprout will add your book to their website/app (if you want them to) so that new reviewers may discover it. Booksprout offers various levels of "freeloader protection" so you can avoid giving your book to those known not to review. Their paid plans also have piracy protection. Lastly, Booksprout keeps track of who's reviewed and lets you see that information.

- **Cons:** The free plan has strict distribution limits. To get unlimited distribution, you'll need a paid plan.
- **I use one of Booksprout's paid plans** (for one or two months only, each time I need it). In the past, I distributed through BookFunnel, but I get better follow-through with Booksprout, since they send reminders *and* I send my own reminders. I've even picked up a small number of new reviewers through their community.

Option 4: BookSirens

- **BookSirens** is a full-featured ARC service for authors and publishers. They have a free plan and various paid plans.
- **Pros:** BookSirens' free plan offers unlimited ARC distribution to readers you directly recruit (such as your newsletter subscribers). At all levels, they provide piracy protection and give you a tool to invite readers to join your mailing list or Facebook group. At all levels, they communicate with reviewers for you. At paid levels, BookSiren will send out your book to reviewers in your genre; and they provide multiple options to deter freebie seekers who don't review. Lastly, BookSirens keeps track of who's reviewed and lets you see that information.
- **Cons:** The biggest con is that they don't provide you with reviewers' email addresses, which makes it difficult for you to communicate directly with reviewers (except those who sign up for your email list).
- **I may try BookSirens' paid plan** to find new reviewers someday. The lack of email addresses will keep me from choosing them as my primary ARC-service provider. However, their free plan has some very nice features. This service is worth considering, especially if you already have email addresses for your ARC readers.

The options above will meet most of your ARC-distribution needs. However, in a few instances, you may need other distribution options.

- Sending **paperback or hardcover ARCs** to any of your reviewers? If using author copies, you'll need a shipping service. If you live in the U.S. and are shipping domestically, the cheapest way to send your books is through USPS Media Mail. (You can't include any "extras," such as bookmarks, in a Media Mail package.)
- Here's another way to ship a **paperback or hardcover ARC**: once your book is published, have Amazon or another retailer ship it as a gift to your reviewer. This is a particularly good option for international reviewers. You can visit the Amazon site that's local to your reviewer (for instance, amazon.co.uk, amazon.ca, or amazon.com.au) and have your book shipped from there to your reviewer, avoiding international shipping.
- **Some Facebook review groups don't allow you to send reviewers to download sites that require email addresses.** That means you can't use Booksprout or BookSirens for ARC readers from these groups. Instead, send each reviewer a private Facebook message. Give them a link to a download page that doesn't require an email address. StoryOrigin, BookFunnel, and ProlificWorks all allow you to set up this type of direct download page.
- **If you're looking for new ARC reviewers, check out a paid service called Hidden Gems.** It doesn't allow you to distribute ARCs to your current readers. However, their service appears to be well run and is popular enough to book up far in advance. If you're looking to grow your team and don't mind paying for it (and

waiting months or even a year to snag a spot on the schedule), check out Hidden Gems.

In Summary: Authors have a wealth of ARC-distribution options. Choose the one that has features you like at a cost that fits your budget.

If you've chosen the distribution service you'll use, excellent! You have one more step to take before you dive into the ARC waters.

PRE-ARC STEP 6: SET UP REVIEW REPORTING

When you track who reviewed your book (and who actually liked it), you'll know who to invite back to review again.

Some ARC-distribution services (such as Booksprout, BookSirens, and StoryOrigin Review Copies) track reviews for you. If you've chosen one of those services, you can skip to the next section of this book.

If you're distributing your ARCs on a site that doesn't track reviews (such as BookFunnel, ProlificWorks, or StoryOrigin Reader Magnets), I suggest setting up a simple Google Form or Jotform where your readers can report their reviews. Here's an example:

The Greatest Novel Ever Review Reporting Form

Full Name:

Email Address:

Review status:

- I reviewed this book.
- I'm unable to review this book.
- I plan to review this book, but I haven't finished yet. (Please fill out this form again after reviewing.)

If you reviewed, how many stars did you give this book? Any number is fine, as long as it's an honest review.

- 1 star
- 2 stars
- 3 stars
- 4 stars
- 5 stars

If you reviewed this book, please provide a link to at least one of your reviews.

―――

In Summary: If your ARC distributor doesn't track your ARC teams' reviews, set up a form for them to report reviews to you.

Congratulations, you're done with your pre-ARC steps! It's time to form an ARC team. First, you'll need to decide how many people to invite. I'll help you think through that on the next page.

HOW BIG AN ARC TEAM SHOULD BE

Before we get into *where* to find ARC readers, let's talk about *how many* you'll want.

Some authors get just enough ARC readers to reach a review goal. Let's say you want ten reviews. You might try to find twenty ARC readers in case half of them fall through.

Why limit the size of your ARC team? Because you're giving your book away to ARC readers . . . for free. You may lose paid sales if you give away too many copies.

Also, by limiting the size of your team, you can be more selective with who you invite, focusing only on your fans or others who love your genre. These readers may be more likely to enjoy your book and review it positively.

Other authors get as many ARC readers as they can.

By getting a lot of ARC readers, these authors start out with more reviews, which gives their book more "social proof" (if most of the reviews are positive).

An author in this camp probably realizes that a lot of ARC readers are freebie seekers who wouldn't actually pay for their book. They gladly give the book away and accept the subsequent reviews, knowing they're not losing many sales.

I take an in-between approach by considering my various audiences and how likely they are to buy my book.

For example, I've worked hard to build a social media presence, and plenty of people I'm connected to have bought my books. I don't want to offer my novels for free to every social media connection, knowing many of them are happy to pay for my work.

However, I've built an email list of fiction readers, most of whom signed up for my newsletter by downloading one of my books for free. A lot of them might never read my books . . . unless they're free. I do market my paid books to subscribers, but I also offer them free ARC copies. I consider my fiction newsletter as a source of reviews more than a source of sales.

In Summary: Set a goal of how many ARC readers to shoot for based on your audience and how many free copies you feel comfortable distributing.

It's time to form your ARC team. Let's discuss where to find readers.

HOW TO FIND ARC READERS

Whether you want a lot of ARC readers or only a few, here are some sources to consider:

Facebook (author page, reader group, personal account, other groups)

- Remember in Part 1 when I suggested you start a **Facebook author page**? If you did that . . . and people have liked your page . . . you're ahead of the game. Post on your author page asking who's interested in getting an early review copy of your book. (In the next section, we'll cover how to ask.)
- An even better source of reviewers is your **Facebook reader group**. Now is the time to start one if you haven't yet.
- You may want to ask your friends on your **personal Facebook account** to join your ARC team (and your reader group). Beware, however—many of your friends may not be readers in your genre.

- Some of my best sources of ARC readers I didn't already know are **genre groups on Facebook that connect authors to ARC readers**. As a YA fantasy author, I always post my books in three groups: YABS (YA Book Stop), Fantasy ARC Readers, and YA Fantasy Readers. You'll need to search for groups in your genre. Let's say you write romance. Search Facebook for "romance ARC" groups, "romance review" groups, and "romance reader" groups. Always check the group's rules and/or get permission from the group admins before posting. If it's the type of group where people get together to talk about books in the genre, you'll want to get involved in the group as a reader so you're not only visiting when you have something to share.

Other social media

- You can post on Twitter or your other social network of choice, asking for ARC readers.

Newsletter

- Offering free ARC copies to newsletter subscribers is a great way to make them feel like "insiders." Concerned about offering your book for free to your whole newsletter? Some authors keep multiple newsletter lists . . . perhaps one for all their potential readers, and another only for readers who've asked to be on an ARC team. (If you don't have a newsletter, check out the article, "0 to 1,000+ mailing list subscribers" on the StoryOrigin blog.)

ARC distribution sites

- As we discussed in "Pre-ARC Step 5: Choose a Distribution Service," some ARC-distribution services connect you to new ARC readers.

Previous ARC readers

- **If you've had ARC teams in the past, reach out to those reviewers.** If you tracked who reviewed and how many stars they gave the book, you may want to only reach out to those who enjoyed your previous work enough to give it at least three (or four) stars.
- You may be asking, *Is it okay to keep someone off my ARC team because they left me a negative review in the past?* Amazon's Community Guidelines say that when "authors and publishers" distribute free review copies, they must not "attempt to influence the review." I don't think that precludes me from carefully choosing ARC readers who are *likely* to review positively, as long as I don't *ask* them to do so. However, rules like this are always open to interpretation. Do what seems right to you.

The personal ask

- Other authors frequently ask me to ARC read for them. Don't hesitate to reach out to personal acquaintances and fellow authors who might enjoy your book.

Instagram

- Instagram is in a class of its own. Your Instagram ARC

team, if you choose to build one, will probably be separate from your other ARC team.
- Instagram has a thriving **Bookstagram community**. Bookstagrammers post gorgeous photos of books—usually hard copies, but sometimes digital.
- I expect most ARC readers to review on Amazon, Goodreads, or Bookbub. Bookstagrammers are different; I'm connecting with them for exposure more than for reviews. Their promotions on their Instagram feed and/or stories are enough for me. Reviews on other sites are a nice bonus though.
- **Some Bookstagrammers will promote your book if you send a free copy. Others require a payment plus a free book.** If they require payment, they should *not* review on Amazon, due to Amazon's review guidelines. Consider your budget carefully. For many authors, sending out physical copies and/or paying Bookstagrammers may be a marketing expense that doesn't make sense.
- **To find Bookstagrammers in your genre, search pertinent hashtags.** For example, if you write YA fantasy, you might search "#fantasy", "#YAFantasy", "#bookstagram #fantasy", etc. When you find Bookstagrammers with great pics and good numbers of followers, pull up their profiles. They'll often list email addresses where you can contact them. Otherwise, you can DM them. (But be careful, Instagram will only let you send the same DM so many times.)
- **In your email and/or DM, include your book cover—** Bookstagram is all about visuals. Ask if you can ship them a copy of your book for them to promote on their feed. If you're only willing to ship to a particular country, make that clear. Here's a potential bonus for those who plan ahead: some Bookstagrammers will help

you promote your cover reveal. You could ask them to promote your book twice: once when you reveal the cover, once when you send them a copy of the book.
- A few more notes about reaching out to Bookstagrammers: **Many will expect a physical copy**, and if you're only willing to offer digital copies, you may not have much luck. Also, you'll want to **keep records** about who you've reached out to, how they responded, their addresses, etc. Spreadsheets are great for keeping all that information in order. Lastly, there are **companies that will organize your Bookstagrammer marketing efforts** for you . . . for a fee, of course.

TikTok: Like Instagram, TikTok has a book-lover community. The hashtag they use is #BookTok, and you can connect with reviewers there. I won't go into detail about this type of promotion, but there are plenty of resources online.

Before we move on, we need to cover an important topic: **who *can't* review your book on Amazon.**

First, I've heard from various sources that **two authors shouldn't directly trade Amazon reviews** with each other. Amazon may consider such reviews to be suspect (since the authors might not be fully honest).

Second, **not everyone can review on Amazon's U.S. site.** They require reviewers to have spent at least $50 on the site within the last year. Plus, it's difficult for Amazon users outside the U.S. to review on amazon.com. (However, international reviewers can review on their own countries' Amazon sites.)

Amazon has other restrictions too. According to the Amazon article, Customer Reviews Guidelines Frequently Asked Questions from Authors (wow, that's a mouthful), **the following people should not review your book on Amazon:**

- An author who "has a personal relationship with" you, "or was involved in the book's creation process (i.e., as a co-author, editor, illustrator, etc.)."
- Any "individuals who share a household with" you.
- Your "close friends."

What happens if you don't follow Amazon's rules? If their algorithms think you're trying to cheat the system, their automated systems may take away some of your reviews or ban certain people from reviewing for you.

Of course, some of these rules are hard to interpret. What makes someone a close friend? At what point does your relationship with another author become personal? I'm not sure, so I share these guidelines with my ARC reviewers and ask them to exclude themselves from reviewing on Amazon if necessary. If you prefer, you can ask specific people who might fit in those categories to only review on sites other than Amazon.

If people in the above categories want to be on your ARC team, can they? Absolutely. Here's how:

- Encourage people who don't meet Amazon review guidelines to review on **Goodreads and/or BookBub**, both of which allow anyone to review.
- **Consider asking authors you're friends with to send their reviews directly to you. You can use those reviews (or quotes from them) as Editorial Reviews on Amazon.** These reviews show up on your book listing right below your book description, and they don't affect your star rating. To add Editorial Reviews to your book's listing, visit Amazon's Author Central website. (You can even format the text of your reviews using the free Amazon Book Description Generator on the Kindlepreneur website.)

In Summary: You've got lots of potential sources of ARC reviewers, from social media to your newsletter. However, it's also important to remember Amazon's guidelines on who shouldn't review your book on their site.

Now that you know where to find potential ARC readers, how do you choose the right ones for your team? We'll address that next.

CHOOSING YOUR ARC READERS

You might be tempted to carefully screen each potential ARC reader, just as you did with alpha and beta readers. However, you need to be careful how you communicate with ARC readers.

You often won't have the same relationship with ARC readers that you have with alphas or betas. **Alpha and beta readers are committed to giving *the author* feedback. ARC readers are committed to giving *the world* feedback.** Some ARC readers, in fact, prefer not to have direct contact with authors. By remaining distant, they feel more comfortable being frank and honest in their reviews. (I do send email reminders to ARC reviewers, but these reminders aren't personalized.)

When choosing ARC readers, I don't do in-depth, individualized screening like I do for potential alpha and beta readers. You can use the following strategies and tools to form a strong team, while keeping distance between yourself and your ARC readers:

- Ask people to only join your team if they enjoy your

genre (more on that in the next section). That way, you'll **target the right readers**.
- As we discussed in the previous section, you can choose to **only personally invite past ARC readers to return if they followed through and enjoyed your previous book(s)**.
- Some distribution sites have automatic systems to help you **avoid "freeloaders"** who won't review. (Check out Booksprout and BookSirens for this feature. See "Pre-ARC Step 5: Choose a Distribution Service," p. 139.)
- StoryOrigin also has an **anti-freeloader** feature, though it's not automatic. They allow you to look at a reviewer's past reliability so you can individually approve or deny every applicant. (This approach still allows authors to remain distant from reviewers, since StoryOrigin handles communications.)
- All the distribution sites allow you to **cap how many people download** your book.

In Summary: Rather than doing an in-depth, individualized screening of every potential ARC reader, you can curate a quality ARC team by targeting those who love your genre and using tools to reduce the number of freeloaders.

Now that you've got strategies on how to find ARC readers, it's time to invite them. Keep reading for tips.

HOW TO ASK FOR ARC READERS

Sometimes, we feel weird about asking people to help us out. But here's the great thing about asking for ARC readers: **you're offering them a gift**. A lot of readers will be *thrilled* when you give them an early copy of your book. Ask confidently!

Your "ask" for ARC readers should include the following elements:

- **Title** (if you've made it public)
- **Cover** (if you've made it public)
- **Genre**
- **Brief description** (if you've got room for it)
- **Release date**
- **A request for** *reviewers,* **not just** *readers*
- **A link** for where they can request a digital ARC. (This is the link you got when you uploaded your book to a distribution site.)

Here's an example of a **"short ask" (appropriate for Twitter)**:

I'm building an ARC team of reviewers for my <u>mystery</u> novel, <u>The Greatest Novel Ever</u>! It's got <u>suspense, humor, and a little romance</u>.

It releases on <u>4-13</u>, and I have a limited number of early, free digital copies. Request one here:

{Insert review link}

Add the book cover as an image, and add a hashtag or two that fits your audience on Twitter. (I'm mostly connected with other authors on Twitter, so if I had space, I'd add #amwriting and/or #WritingCommunity.)

Here's an example of a **"long ask" (appropriate for Facebook, your newsletter, etc.)**:

Subject line [if using email]: <u>Name</u>, want a free review copy of my next novel?

Want a free book to review?

<u>The Greatest Novel Ever</u>, my newest <u>mystery</u> novel, has <u>suspense, humor, and a little romance</u>. I'd love to offer you a free digital ARC (Advance Review Copy).

I'm looking for people who...

- love <u>mystery</u> novels and
- can read and review <u>The Greatest Novel Ever</u> by its release date, <u>April 13</u>.

As an ARC reader, you'll get a digital copy of the book, for free, before its release. You'll even get the chance to enter a competition for who can find the most last-minute typos before the book releases.

I'm distributing ARCs through a website called Booksprout. If you'd like to commit to reading & reviewing, click here to check it out. {link}

If you enjoy this type of book, I hope you'll join the team!

-Your First Name

P.S. I'm giving out a limited number of free copies. If you'd like to snag one, do it soon.

———

If you're publishing Book 2 (or higher) in a series that needs to be read in order, you may wish to specify that you're only asking for ARC readers who've read and/or reviewed the previous book(s).

Also, note that you probably won't get as many ARC readers, or as many reviews in general, after the first book of a series. That's okay. Reviews are most important for the first book of a series. If a reader loves Book 1, they'll probably read Book 2 even if it doesn't have a lot of reviews.

I never say I'm giving someone a book "in exchange for" a review or that a review is *required*. That's because, according to Amazon's Community Guidelines, "Book authors and publishers may . . . provide free or discounted copies of their books to readers, as long as the author or publisher does not require a review in exchange or attempt to influence the review."

In Summary: When asking readers to join your ARC team, describe the ARC process and your book, and encourage them to apply if they enjoy your genre.

To encourage your ARC team to follow through, you'll need to communicate with them well. In the next section, I'll give you practical tips on keeping in touch.

COMMUNICATING WITH ARC READERS

Repeat after me:

PEOPLE ARE BUSY. In fact, as I wrote these words, I remembered I need to review an ARC I received that's now been published. I had to take a break from drafting to write my review . . . and if I hadn't been working on a book about ARC readers, it might've been weeks before I remembered to review!

Our ARC readers are often as busy as we are. That's why, whether we're working with alpha, beta, or ARC readers, we need to communicate well. ARC readers (like me) can easily forget the deadline for reading and reviewing. **You need to remind them.**

Depending which service you choose to distribute your ARCs, either **you or your ARC service will send reminders, or you'll do a combination of both**. I love the *both* option, whether we're talking about cake and ice cream or ARC communication. That's why I use Booksprout, which sends reminders and also provides me with email addresses of those who downloaded my book.

If you're depending on your ARC service to send all your reminders, you can skip to the bottom of this section, where I cover social media communications. Otherwise, keep reading.

Tips for communicating with your ARC readers:

- **Timing:** Communicate with them at least twice during the ARC period, then on release day. A week after release, send a reminder to those who, as far as you know, haven't yet reviewed. (If needed, you can follow up one more time after that.)
- **Privacy:** Don't reveal your reviewers' email addresses to the whole ARC team! Use individual emails, BCC (blind carbon copy), or the email service you use for your author newsletter.

Here's an example of an ARC reminder email. You can use this one for every email *before* release day.

Subject line: Quick reminder to reviewers for The Greatest Novel Ever

Hi, reviewers!

Thank you for signing up to read and review The Greatest Novel Ever.

Here are a few reminders:

- **Release date: Tuesday April 13.** That's just 3 weeks from now.
- **Review links**: Amazon, Goodreads, BookBub {links}. You won't be able to review on Amazon until release day, but I invite early reviews on the other sites.

EARLY READERS CATCH THE WORMS

- **Remember to post links to your reviews** by clicking this link: {link to your book on the ARC site or link to your review-reporting form}. That way, I can **invite you to download an ARC for my next book** when it's available (if you enjoyed this book).
- **Typo hunt:** I'm giving out a prize to whoever finds the most typos and other errors by April 6. Just email me each one you find, including the chapter number and a few words from the sentence. Whoever finds the most valid errors will get a signed paperback copy of my book (or an unsigned copy if you live outside the U.S.) If there's a tie, I'll draw one winner. And *everyone* who submits typos will get a signed bookmark.

Lastly, I'd love to connect with you. You can become an Email Insider here {newsletter sign-up link}, and I invite you to join my Amazing Reader Group on Facebook {link}.

Thanks so much for being an ARC reviewer. Have a great day!

-Your Name

On release day, send an email like this:

Subject line: It's release day for The Greatest Novel Ever!

It's release day for *The Greatest Novel Ever*. I'm thrilled that you joined my ARC team! Your reviews will help more customers find this book.

Here are a few reminders:

- **Review links:** *The book is now available to review everywhere, including Amazon.* Here are your links: Amazon, Goodreads, BookBub {links for all}.
- **Remember to post links to your reviews** by clicking this link: {link to your book on ARC site or link to your review-reporting form}. That way, I can **invite you to download an ARC for my next book** when it's available (if you enjoyed this book).
- **Typo hunt winners:** Congratulations to Sal Sanchez, who won the typo hunt! He'll receive a free signed copy of this book.

Lastly, I'd love to connect with you. You can become an Email Insider here {newsletter sign-up link}, and I invite you to join my Amazing Reader Group on Facebook {link}.

Thanks so much for being an ARC reviewer and for helping me have a successful book launch. I'm off to celebrate!

-Your Name

A week after release day, reach out to anyone who, to the best of your knowledge, hasn't reviewed.

Below is a sample email to send to non-reviewers.

Subject line: Review reminder and request for update

I'm sending this email because you signed up to read and review *The Greatest Novel Ever*, and Booksprout currently shows that you haven't reviewed, or you've reviewed on Booksprout only (without submitting links from your other reviews on Amazon, Goodreads, etc.).

This could mean a few things.

- **Maybe you didn't finish the book.** If that's the case, you're welcome to review whenever you're ready, or you can cancel the review on Booksprout {link} if you don't think you'll get it done.
- **Maybe you reviewed but forgot to put your links on Booksprout.** Just click here to report your reviews {link}.
- **Or you could be having trouble with the Booksprout website.** Feel free to email me with links to your reviews, and I'll mark you as "complete."

If you enjoyed the book and you complete your reviews, I'll invite you to read and review my next book when it's available.

Thanks so much!

-Your Name

While I love using email to communicate with reviewers, sometimes you may need to use social media instead. Here are some examples:

- If you've connected with **reviewers on Instagram or TikTok**, you may need to reach out to them through direct messages.
- Some **book-review sites on Facebook** require authors to communicate with reviewers through direct messages only.

You'll probably never get perfect follow-through from your ARC team, but when you communicate well with them, you can expect at least half of them to leave reviews. If some of your ARC readers enjoy your books enough to keep coming back, your follow-through percentage should increase.

In Summary: By frequently communicating with ARC readers through email, you'll encourage more of them to follow through.

Remember that typo-hunting contest I mentioned? Next, we'll talk about how it works.

ASKING YOUR ARC READERS TO REPORT TYPOS

Throughout this book, we've talked about worms—those squirmy issues, big and small, that keep readers from fully enjoying your novel. Hopefully your alpha and beta readers have caught plenty of worms, from the big ones (like plot and pacing) to the tiny ones (like misplaced commas).

However, a few stubborn worms—typos and errors—remain in most published books. Your book won't be perfect, but ARC readers can help you reach a more realistic goal: excellence.

Here's an example of an ARC reader finding an error I'd missed. I'd written, "He could even sense the soft leather of his shoes, despite the socks between his skin and his feet."

If you don't see the error immediately, don't feel bad. *Dozens* of alpha, beta, and other ARC readers missed it. Peruse it again, and let's all do a community shudder as we picture socks a person wears between their skin and their feet. An ARC reader found this in time for me to update my ebook and paperback files. Unfortunately, I'd already ordered paperbacks for signed copies, so some lucky readers have this typo on their bookshelves.

A lot of reviewers are voracious readers, and some have developed excellent eyes for errors. **I use a typo-hunting contest to encourage my ARC readers to send typos and other errors. Whoever submits the most legitimate errors gets a prize.** Not only does this encourage people to take the time to report what they find, it also makes the process more fun.

Typo-Hunting Contest Tips:

- Give your readers a **contest deadline well before your release date so you have time to make changes**. I suggest setting this deadline for at least a week before the release so that you have time to upload new files.
- **Your first-place prize doesn't need to be big.** A signed paperback of your book is a great incentive. Remember, international shipping is pricey, so have a plan in place in case your winner isn't from your country. You can avoid expensive shipping by ordering a prize from their local Amazon website. (For instance, send an Amazon gift card or an unsigned paperback of your book.)
- **Consider your options if multiple people win.** You may wish to tell your readers in advance that in such a case, you'll do a random drawing to see who wins the prize.
- **In addition to one big prize, consider offering a small prize to *everyone* who submits typos.** For example, you can send a bookmark to each person. (Bonus: international shipping on bookmarks is remarkably affordable.)
- **Ask the winners' permission to share their names** in an email to your ARC team and in the Acknowledgements of your book.

My first typo-hunting contest was a big success. I was in a time crunch and only gave my readers three or four days to enter the typo contest. A few managed to finish the book in time, and others submitted typos late (but soon enough that I could still update my files before publishing).

If you're unsure about your readers' grammatical or style feedback, check into it before changing it. You can ask your editor, look it up in a resource such as *The Chicago Manual of Style*, or join a Facebook group called Ask a Book Editor, where professional editors answer author questions.

In Summary: A typo-hunting contest with a prize is a fun way to ensure your final product is as polished as possible.

We're nearing the end of our section on ARC reading. Let's talk about how to make this process your own.

THE ARC READER PHASE: MAKE IT YOUR OWN

There's not much I'd suggest messing with in this phase. Reader-friendly formatting, simple distribution, and consistent communication are always important during an ARC phase. However, I do have a couple of tweaks you can consider.

- **If you have a book that's likely to sell best in hard copy** (such as a children's picture book or a cookbook), **you may want to primarily use hard-copy ARCs**. You'll need to keep the team size limited unless you have a large budget.
- My author friend Mackenzie Littledale plans to **provide ARC readers with options besides merely reviewing**. For example, you might consider an ARC reader to have fulfilled their commitment if they blog about your book or share it a certain number of times on social media.

In Summary: While you should make the ARC phase your own, don't mess with the basics, like good formatting and consistent communication.

Congratulations, you know how to build a team of ARC readers who will provide you with early reviews!

Let's move on to questions you may have about early reader systems.

PART 4

QUESTIONS & ANSWERS

Q&A: START HERE

This section of the book answers questions you may still have. If you'd like to hop to the questions that are foremost on your mind, flip to these sections:

- Help! What If I'm Overwhelmed? (p. 177)
- Where Do Editors Fit in My Process? (p. 178)
- Do Early Readers Replace Editors? (p. 182)
- What If No One Wants to Read My Book? (p. 185)
- What If My Alpha or Beta Readers Aren't Giving Me Feedback? (p. 187)
- What If My ARC readers Aren't Leaving Reviews? (p. 190)
- Do I Need Sensitivity Readers? (p. 192)
- When Is It Time to "Fire Someone" From an Early Reader Team? (p. 195)
- Should Alpha and/or Beta Readers Review My Finished Book? (p. 197)
- What If I Feel Guilty Asking People to Help Me? (p. 199)

- How Do I Get Over My Fear of Feedback? (p. 201)
- Will Early Readers Steal My Book? (p. 204)
- Can I Send My Book to ARC Readers after It's Published? (p. 207)
- How Can I Thank My Early Readers? (p. 209)

HELP! WHAT IF I'M OVERWHELMED?

If you're new to a lot of the concepts in this book, the information may hit you like a tidal wave.

You don't have to do *all* these steps *at once*. In fact, you don't have to do *all* of them *at all*.

Imperfect early reader teams are a whole lot better than nonexistent early reader teams. So choose a few tips from this book, the ones that resonate most with you. Implement those first. Refine your process as you go, at whatever pace works for you.

As I've said from the beginning, you can make this book your own. If the thought of having a beta reader application sends your heart racing and makes you want to bury your head under the pillow, start a beta team without it. If you don't have time for an ARC phase, eliminate it. The world won't blow up, and neither will your book.

In Summary: Take it one step at a time, and modify as needed. You've got this!

WHERE DO EDITORS FIT IN MY PROCESS?

I've mentioned editing a few times during this book, but you may have questions about how exactly editors fit in.

Note that if you're working with a publishing house, they'll have their own editing process. Your agent or publisher will help you navigate it.

Let's discuss several types of editing and at what points in the process you might utilize editors.

Developmental/content editors

- A developmental or content editor helps you write a book with a **well-structured plot, believable characters, etc.** If your book were a house, a developmental or content editor would ensure your foundation and major systems are functioning properly.
- Consider bringing in a **developmental or content editor after you've made revisions based on alpha reader**

feedback**. By that time, hopefully you have a fairly solid story, and your editor can help you make it stronger.
- However, if you're lost when it comes to story structure, or you have no idea if your concept is any good, **you may prefer to bring in a developmental or content editor before your alpha phase even starts**. As you make changes based on your editor's feedback, you can send portions of the revised manuscript to your alpha readers.
- **In Summary: Developmental/content editing comes before OR after the alpha reading phase.**

Copy/line editors

- **Both copy editors and line editors correct grammar, style, and other errors, and they help make your book more readable.** Continuing with the house metaphor, a copy or line editor ensures your cabinets, floors, and drywall are installed properly.
- Line editors tend to offer a more in-depth service with more readability/rewording suggestions than copy editors. Most authors will choose a copy editor *or* a line editor, and the border between the two types of editing can be a little fuzzy.
- Consider bringing in a **copy or line editor after you've made revisions based on beta reader feedback** so that your editor is making suggestions on a book that's pretty close to complete.
- However, if you know you write with a lot of errors, **you might consider hiring a copy or line editor before you send your manuscript to beta readers**. That way, your beta readers will get a version of the book that's more pleasant to read, and they may be more likely to follow through. (However, if you make a lot of changes based

on beta feedback, you could end up needing another round of copy or line editing, which can get pricey.)
- **In Summary: Copy/line editing comes after the beta reading phase . . . usually.**

Proofreading

- **Proofreaders clean up typos and other grammar, style, and formatting errors shortly before publication.** If your book were a house, proofreaders would fix messed-up paint and sloppy caulk before you move in.
- Consider bringing in a proofreader **right before, during, or after your ARC phase**. It's nice to give your ARC readers a book that's already been proofread, but the timing doesn't always work out for that.
- **In Summary: Proofreading comes before, during, or after your ARC phase.**

Let's discuss one other type of editorial support that goes beyond the words on your page.

Book Coaching

- **Book coaches don't just work with your *book*. They work with *you*.** They give editorial feedback but also help you create and complete a book, supporting you as a person and an author every step of the way. Some book coaches even help you navigate the processes of working with early readers and querying or publishing your novel. Before you hire a coach, communicate with them to find out exactly what services they offer.
- Consider bringing in a book coach **early in your process**, or at any point when **you feel "stuck."**

- **In Summary: Book coaches can help you at all points of your drafting and revision process.**

It would be great if every self-published author could afford multiple rounds of editing for every book. Unfortunately, that's often not in the budget. Evaluate your strengths and weaknesses, and determine where to best spend your editing dollars. And plan ahead! Some editors book their clients many months in advance.

Want to go into more detail on where editing fits in? Appendix 3 (p. 221) gives you a sample early reading, revision, and editing process to help you put this all together.

In Summary: Editors can help you at every stage of your book-creation process.

DO EARLY READERS REPLACE EDITORS?

Editing is often pricey. **To save money, should self-published authors replace editors with strong teams of early readers?**

In a word, *no*.

In a phrase, *not usually*.

Imagine you're starring in an action movie. There's a scene requiring your character to jump from the top of a very tall waterfall into a pool below. (Then you'll defeat the villain and kiss your love interest and live happily ever after . . . until the sequel.)

Here's my question: in this hypothetical movie, *can* you do your own stunt without professional training?

Well, sure. Anyone can jump from a tall height; gravity will ensure you fall.

Maybe the right question is, *should* you do your own stunt without professional training?

Probably not . . . unless, over time, you've developed the skill of taking dangerous leaps from high surfaces.

Editing is the same. *Can* you do your own (with the assistance of early reader volunteers)? Sure. *Should* you do your own? Probably not . . . unless, over time, you've developed significant skills in the editing arena.

A good copy editor will usually suggest hundreds or thousands of changes in one manuscript.

Will betas point out missing words and gleefully inform you that you wrote *their* instead of *there*? Absolutely. But you can't expect even the most detail-oriented betas to make hundreds or thousands of editing notes.

Here's my story of working with (and not working with) a professional editor.

When I started writing books, I already had a keen eye for grammar. I hired a professional copy editor and further developed my grammar and style skills by heeding the feedback she gave me for my first four books. *That took time.*

I've built amazing early reader teams. *That took time too.*

For my second series of novels, I chose not to use a professional editor. These days, by the time my novel goes to beta readers, it's quite polished. My more detail-oriented betas are happy to point out grammatical errors or misused words because there aren't that many of them. Again, *getting to that place took time.*

If you've never jumped from a tall waterfall into a pool far below, I suggest you don't attempt it without a professional to help you. And **if you haven't had time to develop impressive grammar skills and rock-solid early reader teams, I suggest you don't publish without an editor.**

That being said, money is a very real factor. Here are a few ways to make editing more financially accessible:

- **Find a newer editor who's less expensive.** (This can come back to bite you; anyone can call themselves an editor. Get a sample edit first. It may help to ask an experienced author friend to review the sample and determine if the editor is on the right track.)
- **Barter for services.** This isn't an option for everyone. But if you have skills that might help an editor (like graphics or marketing, or even something totally unrelated such as creating handmade items), you may be able to find an editor to swap services with you.
- **Pursue the traditional publishing route by querying agents.** Large, traditional publishers and many small presses provide editing as part of their publication process. The publisher is paid through their cut of the royalties your book eventually earns. (They don't charge you for the editing.) Note, however, that many authors choose to hire editors to help them write better books before querying.
- **Polish your own manuscript as much as you can.** Check out Appendix 4 (p. 223) for self-editing resources, and keep building your early reader teams so they can catch some of your worms.

In Summary: Most authors and their books can greatly benefit from professional editorial support. There are ways to make that support more affordable.

WHAT IF NO ONE WANTS TO READ MY BOOK?

If you're having trouble finding early readers, ask yourself these questions:

- **Do you need to work on your "pitch"?** Search online for "how to write an elevator pitch for a book." You'll find tips on describing your book in such a way that people want to read it.
- **Are you writing in a less popular genre?** If so, it may take longer to find "your readers." Do your best to get a *few* early readers using the tips in this book, and build from there.
- **Are you uncomfortable asking for help, or are you apologizing for asking people to read for you?** Skip forward a few questions to "What If I Feel Guilty Asking People to Help Me?" (p. 199).
- **Did you follow up after you asked people to read?** They may need a couple of gentle nudges.
- **If you're having trouble building an ARC team, is your cover hurting you more than helping you?** Genre-

appropriate covers are immeasurably important when you're trying to connect with the right audience. This starts at the ARC phase (and sometimes earlier, if you're revealing your cover to potential alpha and beta readers).
- **Can you start with a small team?** You may have seen my stories about having huge beta teams. Remember, I didn't start with teams that big, and many authors don't even want huge teams. Be okay with starting small and building from there.

In Summary: If you're having trouble finding early readers, do your best to refine your book, your communication, and/or your expectations.

WHAT IF MY ALPHA OR BETA READERS AREN'T GIVING ME FEEDBACK?

If your alpha or beta readers are backing away from their commitments, it's probably for one or more of these reasons:

They may be too busy. It's normal for a few early readers to back out because they overcommitted. (However, if nearly all your early readers suddenly get busy, some of them probably have deeper reasons for not finishing the book!)

You may not be communicating with your readers often enough. It's easy to drop the ball on frequent communications. But consider how many distractions are fighting for your time. Your readers are in the same boat. Consistent communication may nudge your book nearer to the top of your readers' to-do lists.

The last possibility is the most painful one.

Your book may not be keeping your readers' attention. Nobody's a perfect author, so don't beat yourself up if your book isn't captivating your early readers. One reason you have early readers is to figure out such things before you self-publish or query agents.

Let's talk about how to figure out if the book is the problem.

- **If you have any readers who *are* responding to you, ask them for feedback.** To get honest critiques, you'll need to be honest with them. You might say something like this:

Subject line [if using email]: Quick alpha [or beta] question

Thank you so much for the feedback you've given me.

Unfortunately, I'm not getting responses from most of my other readers. Do you see anything in my book that might be turning readers away? Anything with the plot, pacing, characters, or writing quality?

Please be 100% honest with me. I can handle it! I want to fix my book's major issues, and I hope you can help me track them down.

- **Reach out to your readers who *aren't* responding to you, asking for honest feedback.** Here's some sample verbiage:

Subject line [if using email]: Quick alpha [or beta] question—please respond

Thank you so much for volunteering to be an alpha [or beta] reader! I haven't heard from you lately. I hope everything's okay. Would you mind responding to this email [or message]?

If you've gotten too busy to read, I understand. Just let me know.

And if the book didn't keep your attention, please tell me. You can be 100% honest with me. I can handle it! In fact, your critique might be exactly what I need to make this book better.

Whatever your reasoning, you're "off the hook" if you prefer not to keep reading—no hard feelings. But I'd really love to hear why. Thanks in advance for responding!

If you suspect your book needs major improvements, here are some suggestions:

- **Read books and articles on writing, story structure (see Appendix 1, p. 213), etc.** Writing is a skill you have to hone. You'll never have a *perfect* book to offer to early readers . . . but make sure you're offering them a *good* book.
- **Hire a developmental or content editor and/or a book coach.** Their job is to help you write a book that nails the basics.

You may need to restart your alpha or beta phase once you've reworked the book. That's okay. I've written books that needed lots of reworking. It's easy to miss the mark on the first try.

In Summary: If alpha and beta readers aren't following through, do an honest evaluation of your communication practices and your book.

WHAT IF MY ARC READERS AREN'T LEAVING REVIEWS?

Struggling to get reviews from your ARC readers? Sometimes even the best readers have to back out because life gets in the way. However, if fewer than half of your ARC readers are leaving reviews, consider the following questions:

- **Are you communicating/sending reminders?** I know, I know, I always come back to this. It's that important.
- **Did you give them enough time?** For a full-length novel, try to give ARC reviewers at least a month to read and review. Once your release date passes, encourage stragglers to review whenever they finish the book. Late reviews are still helpful.
- **Did they lose interest in the book?** In the "Communicating With ARC Readers" section (p. 161), I've suggested verbiage for an email you can send to ARC readers who haven't reviewed. If you have a lot of non-reviewers, you might add something like this to your email:

If the book wasn't right for you, I'd love for you to drop me a quick line letting me know why. I value your honesty, and your feedback could be just what I need to help me write a better book next time.

If they don't respond, don't push it. Remember, some ARC readers may prefer not to communicate directly with authors.

If you suspect ARC readers are backing out because the book needs work, check out the suggestions at the end of the previous section. (Work on your writing craft and consider a developmental editor or book coach—for your next book if it's too late for this one.)

In Summary: You may improve ARC follow-through by communicating consistently, giving ARC readers adequate time, and working on the quality of your books.

DO I NEED SENSITIVITY READERS?

You may have heard of sensitivity readers. But what are they, and how do you know if you need them?

According to the article "What are Sensitivity Readers? (And Should Authors Use Them?)" on Reedsy.com's blog, "[s]ensitivity readers are a subset of beta readers who review unpublished manuscripts with the express purpose of spotting cultural inaccuracies, representation issues, bias, stereotypes, or problematic language."

We all sometimes make mistakes in our words, saying insensitive things about people or topics we don't truly understand. If such errors make their way into our writing, we end up hurting our readers and our own reputations. Sensitivity readers help us avoid such painful mistakes.

You may want to consider a sensitivity reader if any of the following apply (though this is not an exhaustive list):

- You're writing about a character who is **LGBTQ+**, and

you don't share your character's sexual or gender identity.
- Some of your characters are of a different **ethnicity** than you; or the characters' **culture** (or the book's cultural setting) differs from yours.
- You have one or more characters with **disabilities** in your book.
- Your book includes descriptions of **traumatic experiences** you don't identify with (such as abuse).

Unlike beta reading, you should always be willing to pay a sensitivity reader for bringing their unique experience and expertise to your manuscript.

You may need one or more sensitivity readers to review your entire book, or you may only ask them to read parts of it. In the manuscript I'm currently working on, I have a couple of characters whose sexual orientations I don't personally identify with. They're secondary characters, so I only asked my sensitivity reader to review the pertinent scenes.

How to find sensitivity readers:

- **Reach out to people you know** (in person or online) who are part of the culture, ethnicity, marginalized group, or identity you're writing about. However, consider whether they know you *too well*. Sometimes people are hesitant to criticize good friends.
- **The directory at WritingDiversely.com** is a fantastic resource listing sensitivity readers, their specialties, and their rates. The website also has a blog that will help you think through the diversity you're bringing to your stories.

Want more advice about writing diverse characters? Check out WritingtheOther.com, an absolutely fantastic resource.

In Summary: Sensitivity readers can help you write about topics and people you don't personally relate to, in ways that are less likely to hurt or cause offense to readers.

WHEN IS IT TIME TO "FIRE SOMEONE" FROM AN EARLY READER TEAM?

You might consider removing someone from your **alpha or beta team** if any of these apply:

- Their critiques are so **negative** that they bring you down as a writer rather than pulling you up. We all need honest feedback, but if someone's words are so harsh that your mental health suffers or you lose the desire to write, that person may not be the best reader for you.
- Their feedback gets **personal**, attacking *you* instead of critiquing your writing.
- They consistently **don't follow through**.

How does this look at each phase?

- **Alpha phase:** In the section of the book called "Removing Inactive Group Members" (p. 62), I've given you a message to send alpha readers who aren't participating. If you're removing someone because of harsh or personal feedback, reword the message as

necessary, keeping it short and polite. This is kind of like a breakup. There's no way to avoid it being awkward, but you can't let that stop you from getting out of a toxic relationship.
- **Beta phase:** If you need to "fire" a beta reader, you can accomplish this by not inviting them to beta again and/or declining when they apply. (You may need to keep them off your ARC team too.)

Consider not inviting an **ARC reader** to return for future books if either of the following apply:

- They **didn't follow through** with a previous ARC commitment. (If they gave you a good reason for it, consider giving them a second chance.)
- Their previous **ARC review was negative**, and you don't have any reason to think they'll like your next book any better. (For more details on Amazon's guidelines regarding this situation, head back to "How to Find ARC Readers," p. 150.)

In Summary: It's good to remove people from early reader teams if their feedback is abusive or overly negative, or if they consistently don't follow through.

SHOULD ALPHA AND/OR BETA READERS REVIEW MY FINISHED BOOK?

Because alpha and beta readers have read your book, you may wonder if you should ask them to review it on Amazon, Goodreads, or other sites. However, **I don't *ask* alpha or beta readers to review unless they join my ARC team.** A review of an early version of my book might not accurately represent the book to potential purchasers, because I always make significant changes as I revise.

If an alpha or beta reader *asks me* if I want them to review, I leave the decision up to them. I never want to give too much guidance to reviewers since I value their honesty.

Some of my beta readers have given my novels positive ratings and reviews, based on the beta version they read. In my experience, most alpha and beta readers understand it would be unfair to negatively review an early version of a book.

What if an early reader gives you a negative review based on worms you've since removed from your manuscript? It's generally considered a bad "look" when authors respond to reviews, and if you have plenty of positive reviews to balance out the negative one, I'd suggest you leave it be. If you *don't* have positive reviews to balance it out, you can consider leaving an upbeat comment thanking them for reading early and letting them know you revised the book after they read it . . . but even that is *very* iffy. Use your own judgment.

In Summary: While I don't ask alpha and beta readers to review, I don't try to stop them from it.

WHAT IF I FEEL GUILTY ASKING PEOPLE TO HELP ME?

Many authors feel guilty asking people to join their early reader teams. It can be a tough mental roadblock to get past.

My first piece of advice is this: **be a generous author**. In the "Pros and Cons of Asking Fellow Authors to be Early Readers" section (p. 25), I talk about having a **pay-it-forward mentality**. If you're offering your time to other authors (by joining beta and ARC teams, for example), you may find it easier for you to ask other people to lend their time to you.

Here's something else to keep in mind: **being an early reader is a privilege**. You're giving someone a free early copy of your book, and you're even taking their opinions into account. Sure, some people might agree to be early readers because they want to do you a favor. However, most early readers who stick around for *multiple books* probably enjoy the process.

Despite all that, **sometimes asking for early readers feels really uncomfortable.** For this book, I had to build teams mostly from scratch, since I couldn't expect my fiction readers to be interested in a nonfiction book geared towards authors. Asking wasn't easy.

Like so many uncomfortable things in life, sometimes we have to acknowledge that asking is hard, then **do the hard thing**. Ask for readers with as much confidence as you can drum up, looking forward to the day when it's easier than it is now.

In Summary: Asking people to join your early reader teams can be hard, but you and your work are worthy of being supported.

HOW DO I GET OVER MY FEAR OF FEEDBACK?

If you have a "thick skin" and aren't afraid of feedback, good for you! You can skip this part.

Still here? Let's huddle up and be honest with each other.

Negative feedback is hard to take. I'm a sensitive soul, and I doubt I'll ever read a difficult critique and let out a long, contented sigh afterward.

I'll also *never* tell another author to grow a thicker skin. We sensitive authors bring our sensitivity (and hopefully empathy) to our writing, using it to create emotionally rich characters and scenes.

But we have to find ways to be open to negative feedback even when it hurts. Here are a few tips that have helped me:

- **Find someone you can be honest with.** Please don't log onto Twitter to post a screenshot of your one-star review or negative beta feedback, complaining about the person who gave it to you. Publicly shaming people who critique your work is a bad strategy. Instead, find someone (a good friend, supportive family member, therapist, or trusted member of an online writing community) and tell them privately how you truly feel. Does it hurt? Are you afraid you suck as an author? Are you angry, depressed, embarrassed? *Say it.* Don't let that stuff eat you up inside. Accept the kind words you get from your supportive friend, and keep going.

- **Take a break.** Step away from the feedback. Do something that relaxes you and makes you happy. Engage in activities that will help you love your book again, like making aesthetics (collections of images that represent your characters and settings), creating music playlists that fit your story, or even writing short pieces of "fanfiction" within your story world.
- **Thank the alpha or beta reader who gave you the feedback (unless they're hateful).** Switching to a mindset of gratitude may help you feel better about the critique. I don't suggest responding to negative reviews, however. Reviews are for readers. Respect the reviewer/reader relationship by not inserting yourself into it more than you need to.
- **Ask your early reader for clarification** if a particular critique doesn't make sense to you or you can't seem to get past your negative reaction to it. Sometimes such conversations help us understand the feedback better and respond to it more productively.
- **Dive into revisions.** When I get negative feedback that hurts, I give myself time to feel the pain and share it with others. Then I dive into revisions, and something magical happens: the critiques hurt a lot less when I see my manuscript improving.
- If the negative critique comes from an alpha or beta reader, repeat these words (out loud if possible): **"I'd**

rather hear this critique from an early reader than a reviewer."

- **If you get a negative public review, learn from it if you can.** A critique that says nothing more than "I hated this book" doesn't help you. But specific critiques (like "The beginning of this book was slow" or "I didn't find the dialogue believable") are often (painful) gifts. Is it hard hearing such feedback on an already published work? Absolutely. But when you use that critique to make your next book better, at least you've gotten something good out of it. (By the way, you may get positive reviews that go something like this: "This book was great, but . . ." My writing has improved when I've taken heed of the gentle criticism after the "but.")

In Summary: Getting negative feedback is hard. Be honest about your pain. Then do something positive with it.

WILL EARLY READERS STEAL MY BOOK?

If someone steals your work and claims they wrote it, that's plagiarism. Please do everything legally possible to stop them. Thankfully, most people won't risk plagiarizing entire books. It's too easy for authors to prove they wrote the words first.

Piracy, on the other hand, is incredibly common. Book pirates steal digital books and distribute them without permission, usually giving them away for free on shady websites.

I used to worry more about piracy than I do now. I read an article titled "Publishing Tip: Why Authors Shouldn't Worry About Piracy" by Robert Kroese on Joanna Penn's blog. It shifted my view on piracy, and it's not something I worry about much anymore. Kroese makes two main points:

- **Most people who download pirated books wouldn't have purchased those books,** so piracy probably isn't costing you much money.
- **Pirated books can increase your visibility.**

Check out the article for a more in-depth exploration of the topic.

Does that mean piracy isn't a problem? Absolutely not. I don't like knowing that people are stealing my hard work, and while I choose not to worry about piracy, I respect and appreciate those who fight the good fight against it. Here are some ways to **reduce the likelihood of your books being pirated** by early readers:

- Check out these sections: "Providing Book Files to Readers" (p. 43) and "Pre-ARC Step 5: Choose a Distribution Service" (p. 139). Some of the services that allow you to distribute your ePub, mobi, and PDF files have **anti-piracy measures** in place.
- **Require your early readers to sign an agreement not to steal your files.** This is part of my beta application. If you'd like, you can require the same thing from alpha and ARC readers.

We won't go deep into copyright law, as I'm not an attorney, and laws vary between countries. However, I'll tell you this: in the United States, your work is considered copyrighted as soon as you write it, even if you haven't registered the copyright. That means those typo-filled pages you give your ARC readers are already copyrighted. It's not legal for someone to distribute your work without your permission at *any* phase of your writing process.

Does sharing your work with others open you up to piracy? Yes. But consider this: Before you publish, you have control over who you show your work to. That's usually *not* when a book is pirated.

Usually, a book is pirated after it's published, when absolutely anyone can access it by simply purchasing an affordable copy. If your book resonates with enough readers, it will almost certainly be pirated. That's the nature of digital files. So I suggest you do your best to put trustworthy people on your early reader teams, and don't let fear of piracy prevent you from getting feedback when it matters most: *before* you publish.

In Summary: While I don't personally lose sleep over early readers pirating my books, there are steps you can take to make such a scenario less likely. Piracy is most likely to happen after you publish, so you shouldn't let fear of it keep you from getting early feedback.

CAN I SEND MY BOOK TO ARC READERS AFTER IT'S PUBLISHED?

An ARC (Advance Review Copy) is, by definition, sent in advance of publication. However, **some authors send out free RCs (Review Copies) after publication.** If you decide to try this, you can use the same distribution service you used for your ARCs. (See "Pre-ARC Step 5: Choose a Distribution Service," p. 139.)

If your ebook is in **KDP Select/Kindle Unlimited**, it's probably best not to distribute RCs after publication. According to the KDP Select page on the KDP website, one of the requirements of being in KDP Select is to "make your Kindle book exclusive to the Kindle Store for the KDP Select enrollment period (90-days)."

That page on Amazon's site used to list an exception to the exclusivity rule: they said authors could email copies of KDP Select books to professional reviewers in an effort to get feedback on editing and such. Many authors thus felt it was fine to send out RCs of their KDP Select books after publication. However, I can no longer find that exception on Amazon's site.

Here's what three ARC distributors say about this:

- BookSirens says it *might* **be okay** to use their service with published books that are enrolled in KDP Select.
- Booksprout says it's *not* **okay**.
- StoryOrigin advises you to **purchase and gift a Kindle copy of your book to potential reviewers,** which will keep you within the KDP Select terms. (Check out the article "Buy Kindle Books for Others" on the Amazon Help website. You can even save money by purchasing multiple gift copies of your ebook when it's on sale. Then you can give them away at a later date.)

My policy? Once I've published a book, whether it's in KDP Select or not, I no longer offer free copies to reviewers. At that point, I want paid readers. (Plus, most of my books *are* in KDP Select, and I want to be careful to stay within their terms.) If I had a book that wasn't in KDP Select, and it didn't have many reviews, I'd consider giving away copies in a *short-term push* for reviews.

In Summary: It's fine to give away review copies after publication, unless you're in KDP Select.

HOW CAN I THANK MY EARLY READERS?

Here are some ways to make sure your early readers feel appreciated:

- **Thank them privately.** When alpha and beta readers give you feedback, be gracious by thanking them individually. You'll also want to include expressions of gratitude in your groupwide ARC emails.
- **Thank them publicly.** I list my alpha and beta readers on my book's Acknowledgements page, with their permission. Note that I don't list ARC readers in my Acknowledgements. As I said before, ARC readers are reviewing for other readers, rather than for me. (I do, however, list the winners of the typo-hunting contest, with their permission.)
- **Give them "extras."** I once sent bookmarks to all my beta readers, and I plan to do that again. I dream of a day when it fits my budget to send signed copies of my books to all my alpha and beta readers. Don't ever give anything except a copy of your book to ARC readers

who are reviewing on Amazon. You're not supposed to "pay" them. (I do send them bookmarks if they send me typos, since I'm thanking them for that service, not for their review. This may be a "gray area," so consider carefully whether you feel comfortable with it.)

In Summary: Show appreciation to your early readers, both publicly and privately.

CONCLUSION

Congratulations, you now have the tools to build effective teams of early readers!

You've digested a lot of information. Take it one step at a time, and remember these principles:

- **Set clear expectations.**
- **Communicate often and effectively.**
- **Keep working to write better books.**
- **Just as you're asking others to be generous with their time, be generous with yours.**

Before you go, I'd like to offer you a few more resources to help you along the way.

If you haven't yet claimed your free resource pack, now is the time! Visit this link to get your editable templates and subscribe to my Author Resources newsletter:

carolbethanderson.com/earlyreaders

Want to discuss your alpha, beta, and ARC processes with other authors? You're invited to share ideas and troubleshoot in the *Early Readers Catch the Worms* Facebook group.

Lastly, check out the **Appendices** on the following pages to go into more depth on these topics:

- Appendix 1: Story Structure Resources (p. 213)
- Appendix 2: File Formatting Options (p. 215)
- Appendix 3: A Sample Early Reading, Revision, and Editing Process (p. 221)
- Appendix 4: Self-Editing and Revision Resources (p. 223)
- Appendix 5: Useful Websites (p. 225, a list of links I've shared throughout the book)

Write your story . . . smash your worms . . . and publish an amazing novel.

I hope you enjoyed this book—thank you for reading it! I'd love for you to write a short review on Amazon/or Goodreads so more readers can find this book. Thanks in advance.

Hope to see you in our *Early Readers Catch the Worms* Facebook group, where we discuss our early reader processes.

-Beth

APPENDIX 1: STORY STRUCTURE RESOURCES

These resources will help you learn to craft a well-told story.

- "The Secrets of Story Structure (Complete Series)," a free blog series by K.M. Weiland

- "How to Outline a Novel," a blog post by Sean Platt (includes a fantastic forty-chapter outlining tool)

- *Creating Character Arcs: A Masterful Author's Guide to Uniting Story Structure (Helping Writers Become Authors)* by K.M. Weiland

- *Save the Cat! Writes a Novel: The Last Book on Novel Writing You'll Ever Need* by Jessica Brody

- *Book Craft: How to write books readers love, from first draft to final polish* by Derek Murphy

APPENDIX 1: STORY STRUCTURE RESOURCES

- *The Secrets of Story: Innovative Tools for Perfecting Your Fiction and Captivating Readers* by Matt Bird

APPENDIX 2: FILE FORMATTING OPTIONS

REEDSY

Reedsy offers a free online book writing/formatting tool where you can draft your book (or import your Word file) and export to mobi, ePub, and print-ready PDF formats.

Pros

- Beautiful results
- Modern, simple interface that's easy to use
- Free

Cons

- Fewer customization options than Vellum or Calibre

Best for: Authors who want a free, fairly flexible option for drafting and/or formatting

APPENDIX 2: FILE FORMATTING OPTIONS

DRAFT2DIGITAL

Draft2Digital is an ebook distribution platform that allows you to upload Word documents and export them to mobi, ePub, and print-ready PDF formats.

Pros

- Free, whether you use them to distribute a book or not
- Quite a few style options

Cons

- Dated user interface that's not always intuitive
- You're required to fill out all the pertinent fields as if you're using Draft2Digital to distribute your book, even if you're only using them for formatting.
- You can't edit a formatted manuscript on their website, so your Word document must properly use page breaks, headings to indicate chapter names, etc. (See "Notes" below.)
- Some of their style options look less than professional, in my opinion.

Best for: Authors who have simple manuscripts, well-formatted in Word, and who plan to use Draft2Digital to distribute ebooks on various platforms.

KDP

Through **KDP** (Kindle Digital Publishing), self-publishers publish directly to Amazon. As part of the process of listing a book there, you can upload a Microsoft Word doc, then export as mobi and HTML files (by clicking "Preview on your computer").

APPENDIX 2: FILE FORMATTING OPTIONS

You can then use a free converter such as Convert.io to make an ePub file.

Pros

- Free
- Same website you may use to sell your books (if you're self-publishing)

Cons

- You can't edit your formatted manuscript on their website, so your Word document must properly use page breaks, headings to indicate chapter names, etc. (See "Notes" below.)
- You'll need to create your own Table of Contents.
- KDP doesn't export ePubs. Instead, you'll need to download the HTML file and use a free conversion site such as Convert.io to convert to ePub.
- KDP doesn't export PDFs. You can export your Word file as a PDF instead through the "Save As" command.

Best for: Authors whose manuscripts are well-formatted in Word and who plan to use KDP to sell ebooks.

CALIBRE

Calibre is free, open-source software you can use to generate mobi and ePub files.

Pros

- Free
- More flexibility with how the final product looks than many other programs provide

APPENDIX 2: FILE FORMATTING OPTIONS

Cons

- Dated-looking user interface
- Big learning curve (Google and YouTube are your friends)
- You'll need to create your own Table of Contents.
- Not the best for PDF. (Better to export your Word file as a PDF instead through the "Save As" command.)

Best for: Authors who are very tech-minded and want a flexible formatting solution

SCRIVENER

Scrivener is software used to organize and write books. You can use Scrivener to generate mobi, ePub, and print-ready PDF files.

Pros

- Plan, draft, and format all in one place.
- Affordable software

Cons

- Your formatted manuscript may not be as "pretty" as it would be with some other options.
- While the software is affordable, it's not free.

Best for: Authors already writing their books in Scrivener

ATTICUS

Atticus is software arriving in 2021 that works on Mac, Windows, Linux, and Chromebook. It generates ePub and print-ready PDF files from Microsoft Word files. You can then use a free converter like Convert.io to make a mobi file (to distribute directly to your early readers). You also have the option of drafting your book within Atticus.

Pros

- One-time cost
- Works on various platforms

Cons

- As of 2021, it's new software, and it will be some time before all its planned features are in place.
- It's one of the more expensive options.

Best for: Authors who want a flexible formatting option and plan to publish several books

VELLUM

Vellum is software that generates mobi, ePub, and print-ready PDF files from .docx (Microsoft Word) files.

Pros

- Beautiful results
- Many formatting/customization options
- Easy to use
- One-time investment (with free updates)

Cons

- Mac only (though some authors use a service called MacinCloud to run it on their PCs)

APPENDIX 2: FILE FORMATTING OPTIONS

- Pricey
- While it offers far more customization options than Reedsy or Draft2Digital, it does have its limits.

Best for: Self-publishing Mac users who want flexible, easy-to-use software and don't mind the one-time investment

NOTES

The **Draft2Digital** and **KDP** methods require you to have a document that's perfectly formatted in Microsoft Word. And all the methods that involve uploading a Word document will require much less "tweaking" if your Word document is formatted well.

I have a video tutorial to help you with this Word formatting. You can find it in the blog post titled "Formatting a Novel in Microsoft Word" at carolbethanderson.com.

The Draft2Digital article, "The Pocket Guide to eBook Layout," also gives Word formatting tips.

If you use the **KDP** or **Calibre** methods, you'll need to create your own Table of Contents. The Microsoft Support article, "Insert a table of contents," shows you how.

I have a Mac, and I use Vellum. (I formatted this book with it). It's generally simple to use, and my books look professional. To me, it's worth the price. If Reedsy's free formatter or Atticus's paid software had been available at the time I purchased, I might have used one of those instead.

Some of this information may change as time passes. You can review post-publication changes to the resources in this book at carolbethanderson.com/updates.

APPENDIX 3: A SAMPLE EARLY READING, REVISION, AND EDITING PROCESS

Every writer has their own process for getting from first to final draft. Below is a sample that's based on my own publishing experience and that of other authors.

1. **Drafting/alpha reading:** Write the first draft. Send one-quarter of the book at a time to alpha readers.
2. **Revisions based on alpha feedback:** Thoroughly revise each chapter. Add, reorganize, and remove chapters and scenes as necessary.
3. **Developmental or content editing**
4. **Revisions based on editor feedback:** Revise as needed. Once a chapter is revised, listen to your computer read it. (Search online for how to do this; it varies according to which software and operating system you're using.) Put each chapter through an editing program such as ProWritingAid, Grammarly, or AutoCrit.
5. **Read through the entire book on a handheld device:** Reading on a different device helps you see things you didn't notice on your computer. Either read when you're

near your computer, making changes as you go; or take notes on your device as you read, and make changes afterward. While revising, keep Track Changes on (if working in Microsoft Word) so that when you're done revising, you can check your revisions before finalizing them.
6. **Beta reading**
7. **Revise based on beta feedback:** Again, use Track Changes, and check your changes before finalizing them. You may wish to repeat all of Step 5 (reading on a handheld device) after completing your major changes.
8. **Copy or line editing**
9. **Revise based on editor feedback:** Use Track Changes, and check your changes before finalizing them.
10. **Professional proofreading**
11. **Revise based on proofreader feedback:** Use Track Changes, and check your changes before finalizing them.
12. **ARC reading:** Include a typo-and-error-hunting contest.
13. **Correct errors found by ARC readers:** Use Track Changes, and check your changes before finalizing them.
14. **Publish**

Remember, these are just suggestions. Your process will probably look different.

APPENDIX 4: SELF-EDITING AND REVISION RESOURCES

Robust self-editing and revision skills will help you write better books, which could lead to more of your early readers following through. Your copy editor may also charge less for a manuscript with few errors.

- *Self-Editing for Fiction Writers, Second Edition: How to Edit Yourself Into Print* by Renni Browne and Dave King

- *Self-editing for Self-publishers: Incorporating—A Style Guide for Fiction* by Richard Bradburn

- *Fix Your Damn Book!: How to Painlessly Edit Your Novels & Stories* by James Osiris Baldwin

- *Revising Your Novel: First Draft to Finished Draft Omnibus: A step-by-step guide to a better novel* by Janice Hardy

- "25 Self-Editing Tips for Indie Authors (and 8 amateur

APPENDIX 4: SELF-EDITING AND REVISION RESOURCES

writing mistakes to avoid)" by Derek Murphy at creativindie.com

- "How to Edit a Book 101: Checklist and Tips for Self-Editing" at blog.reedsy.com

APPENDIX 5: USEFUL WEBSITES

Below are the various links/resources I've included elsewhere in the book. (I'm not including those listed in the other appendices.)

These links in clickable format will be included in your resource pack. (See second URL below.)

INTRODUCTION

Updates to the information in this book:

- https://www.carolbethanderson.com/updates/

Sign up for a resource pack of editable resources and templates:

- https://www.carolbethanderson.com/earlyreaders

APPENDIX 5: USEFUL WEBSITES

PART 1: ALPHA READERS

Free-for-commercial-use images:

- Pexels https://www.pexels.com/
- Pixabay https://pixabay.com/

Free image editor:

- Canva https://www.canva.com

Facebook reader group ideas:

- "How to Create, Cultivate, & Maintain an Active Author/Reader Group on Facebook!" by Samantha A. Cole http://oneauthortoanother.com/2018/09/21/371/

Manuscript formatting options:

- Reedsy https://reedsy.com/write-a-book/book-writing-software-faq
- Draft2Digital https://www.draft2digital.com/blog/draft2digital-introduces-professional-quality-ebook-templates/
- KDP https://kdp.amazon.com/en_US/bookshelf (used in conjunction with Convert.io to convert HTML to ePub) https://convertio.co/html-epub/
- Calibre https://calibre-ebook.com/
- Scrivener https://www.literatureandlatte.com/scrivener/overview
- Vellum https://vellum.pub/ (used in conjunction with MacinCloud for PC users) https://www.macincloud.com/

APPENDIX 5: USEFUL WEBSITES

Sites that help you provide book files to your readers:

- StoryOrigin https://storyoriginapp.com/
- ProlificWorks https://www.prolificworks.com/
- BookFunnel https://bookfunnel.com/

Ask a Book Editor (Facebook group where authors get free advice on grammar, etc. from editors):

- https://www.facebook.com/groups/1754530731241951

How to take and export Kindle notes:

- https://www.carolbethanderson.com/how-to-take-and-export-kindle-notes/

Organizing alpha and beta feedback:

- https://www.carolbethanderson.com/organizing-alpha-and-beta-reader-feedback/

Starting and growing an author newsletter:

- "0 to 1,000+ mailing list subscribers" https://storyoriginapp.com/blog/email-marketing-guide

PART 2: BETA READERS

Grammar-checking software:

- ProWritingAid https://prowritingaid.com/
- Grammarly https://www.grammarly.com/
- AutoCrit https://www.autocrit.com

APPENDIX 5: USEFUL WEBSITES

YouTube tutorials on Microsoft Word Track Changes:

- https://www.youtube.com/results?search_query=track+changes+word

Forms websites (for your beta application and feedback form)

- Google Forms https://docs.google.com/forms/
- Jotform https://www.jotform.com/

Beta reader websites/apps:

- **Beta Books app** https://betabooks.co/
- **Beta Reader app** https://betareader.io/

PART 3: ARC READERS

Cover critique groups on Facebook:

- Indie Cover Project https://www.facebook.com/groups/20CoversTo50k
- The Cover Clinic https://www.facebook.com/groups/thecoverclinic

"Using Both KDP & IngramSpark for Paperback Printing":

- https://carolbethanderson.com/using-both-ingramspark-and-kdp-for-paperback-printing/

BookBub links:

- BookBub Partners (authors) signup https://partners.bookbub.com/

APPENDIX 5: USEFUL WEBSITES

- Claim your book on BookBub https://partners.bookbub.com/my_books?page=add

Goodreads links:

- Apply to be a Goodreads Author https://www.goodreads.com/author/program
- Goodreads Librarian Group (post here if your book doesn't show up on your profile) https://www.goodreads.com/topic/group_folder/59?group_id=220

Other book retail/review sites:

- Barnes & Noble https://www.barnesandnoble.com
- Kobo https://www.kobo.com
- Apple Books https://www.apple.com/apple-books/

Note-taking apps:

- Google Keep https://www.google.com/keep/
- Microsoft OneNote https://www.onenote.com

How to organize links:

- https://www.carolbethanderson.com/author-resources-organize-your-marketing-links/

ARC distribution sites:

- BookFunnel https://authors.bookfunnel.com/help/send-arcs/
- ProlificWorks https://www.prolificworks.com/uses
- StoryOrigin Review Copies https://storyoriginapp.com/tutorials/creating-review-copies

APPENDIX 5: USEFUL WEBSITES

- StoryOrigin Reader Magnets https://storyoriginapp.com/tutorials/creating-reader-magnets
- Booksprout https://booksprout.co/pricing
- BookSirens https://booksirens.com/pricing
- Hidden Gems https://www.hiddengemsbooks.com/

Forms websites (for your review-reporting form):

- Google Forms https://docs.google.com/forms/
- Jotform https://www.jotform.com/

TikTok marketing resources:

- https://www.google.com/search?q=how+to+use+tiktok+as+an+author

Amazon review guidelines:

- https://www.amazon.com/gp/help/customer/display.html/ref=amb_link_1?ie=UTF8&nodeId=201602680&pf_rd_m=customer-reviews-guidelines

More Amazon review guidelines:

- https://www.amazon.com/gp/community-help/customer-review-guidelines-faqs-from-authors

Amazon Author Central (to input Editorial Reviews):

- https://author.amazon.com/home

QUESTIONS & ANSWERS

Formatting site for Amazon Editorial Reviews:

APPENDIX 5: USEFUL WEBSITES

- https://kindlepreneur.com/amazon-book-description-generator/

Google results for "how to write an elevator pitch for a book":

- https://www.google.com/search?q=how+to+write+an+elevator+pitch+for+a+book

"What are sensitivity readers?" blog post:

- https://blog.reedsy.com/sensitivity-readers/

Directory of sensitivity readers:

- https://www.writingdiversely.com/directory

"Publishing Tip: Why Authors Shouldn't Worry About Piracy" blog post by Robert Kroese:

- https://www.thecreativepenn.com/2017/02/23/piracy/

Amazon's KDP Select:

- https://kdp.amazon.com/en_US/help/topic/G200798990

What ARC-distribution services say about giving away review copies of your KDP Select book:

- BookSirens https://support.booksirens.com/article/12-does-this-play-nice-with-kdp-select-kindle-unlimited-terms
- Booksprout https://help.booksprout.co/article/78-faq-

APPENDIX 5: USEFUL WEBSITES

- can-i-use-booksprout-for-arcs-if-im-in-kdp-select-kindle-unlimited
- StoryOrigin https://storyoriginapp.com/review-copies-in-kdp-select

Buying copies of your Kindle book to give to reviewers:

- https://www.amazon.com/gp/help/customer/display.html?nodeId=GVWGP284MQ6ZRM59

CONCLUSION

***Early Readers Catch the Worms* Facebook Group:**

- http://www.facebook.com/groups/earlyreaderscatchtheworms/

If you're reading this, you love to finish things. You're my kind of person! Thanks for flipping all the way to the end of *Early Readers Catch the Worms*. Will you write a short review on Amazon and/or Goodreads? It'll help other readers find this information. Thanks in advance!

Hope to see you in our *Early Readers Catch the Worms* Facebook group, where we discuss our early reader processes.

-Beth

ACKNOWLEDGEMENTS

Whether I'm creating new worlds or getting down and dirty with writing and publishing details, I don't ever write books alone. (If you read even a few pages of this book, that probably doesn't surprise you!)

My alpha team for this book was seriously amazing. Their guidance was massively helpful as they asked questions, pointed out oddly organized sections, and made all sorts of fantastic suggestions. Thank you from the bottom of my heart to Danielle Ancona; Yvette Bostic; J.R. Bournville; MK Clark; Adrian Hall, action hero; Avery Kingston; Riv Rains; The troll; and Deborah Wynne.

I also had an incredible beta team. Their incisive feedback led me to make many changes to clarify and expand on the information in these pages. It's a far better book due to them. My deepest gratitude goes to Bug, Jaime Dill (much of the "Take a break" advice in the Q&A about fear of feedback came directly from her), Dr. Celia Brayfield, Maria Farb, Julie C. Gilbert, Liz

Henderson, Victoria Kelly, Deb Linne, Roslyn Muir, J.C. Paulson, David Allen Voyles, and Toni Wall.

Thank you to the ARC readers who found my typos! A few worms always wriggle through, and I'm glad you have such sharp eyes. Special congratulations and gratitude go to James Taylor-Loftus (J.P. Priestley) and Alicia Williams, who won my typo-hunting contest.

Twitter #WritingCommunity, you're amazing! Thank you for being my friends and supporters. In particular, my gratitude goes out to Eden Campbell for sharing her critique-group experience using Google Docs; romance author, Cass Michaels for tips on using Google Docs and giving out sample chapters; and Mackenzie Littledale for sharing her experiences with using paper copies for beta readers and giving out sample chapters.

Lastly, thank you to God and my family, who keep me going in these challenging times.

-Carol Beth Anderson
Leander, Texas
2021

ABOUT THE AUTHOR

Carol Beth Anderson is a native of Arizona and now lives in Leander, TX, outside Austin. She has a husband, two kids, a miniature schnauzer, and more fish than anyone knows what to do with. Besides writing, she loves baking sourdough bread, knitting, eating cookies-and-cream ice cream, and spending way too much time on Twitter. Beth is the author of the Sun-Blessed Trilogy, The Magic Eaters Trilogy, and *The Curio Cabinet: A Collection of Miniature Stories*.

Find Beth on Facebook, BookBub, and Goodreads, all under the name Carol Beth Anderson. She's also on Twitter and Instagram as @CBethAnderson.

www.ingramcontent.com/pod-product-compliance
Lightning Source LLC
Chambersburg PA
CBHW030321100526

44592CB00010B/523